# The Power of the JUBILEES

### J.S. Whiteley & G.W. Morrison

Tel. 0115 961 1066

**Book Law Publications**

www.booklaw.co.uk

ISBN 978 1 909625 17 4

Published by:
Book Law Publications
382 Carlton Hill
Nottingham
NG4 1JA

Printed by:
The Amadeus Press
Cleckheaton
BD19 4TQ

*Title page* The 'up' "Thames-Clyde Express" approaches Ais Gill summit on 27th March 1960 in the charge of No. 45565 *Victoria*, which it must have worked many times, as it was based at Leeds, Holbeck depot for over 20 years. It finished its working career still based in the West Riding of Yorkshire, allocated to Low Moor depot, Bradford, at the time of withdrawal in January 1967.

*R. H. Leslie*

A study of No. 45593 *Kolhapur* on the turntable inside Holbeck depot at Leeds. The locomotive is in unlined green livery, and was in clean external condition as it was frequently used on specials during 1967, as well as working over the Settle & Carlisle line on Scottish relief trains. The gloomy dilapidated condition of the shed is clearly seen in this picture taken on 15th July 1967. Happily the locomotive is now preserved.

*John Whiteley*

## Summary of Locomotives Built – Total 191:

| BR Nos | Builder | Work's/Builder's No. | LMSR Lot No. | Year Built |
|---|---|---|---|---|
| 45552 – 45556 | LMSR Crewe | 163 – 167 | 97 | 1934 |
| 45557 – 45593 | North Bristol Locomotive Co. | 24115 – 24151 | 118 | 1934 |
| 45594 – 45606 | North Bristol Locomotive Co. | 24152 – 24164 | 118 | 1935 |
| 45607 – 45646 | LMSR Crewe | 163 – 207 | 112 | 1934 |
| 45647 – 45654 | LMSR Crewe | 208 – 215 | 112 | 1935 |
| 45655 – 45662 | LMSR Derby | – | 113 | 1934 |
| 45663 – 45664 | LMSR Derby | – | 113 | 1935 |
| 45665 – 45681 | LMSR Crewe | 263 – 279 | 121 | 1935 |
| 45682 – 45694 | LMSR Crewe | 280 – 292 | 121 | 1936 |
| 45695 – 45742 | LMSR Crewe | 293 – 340 | 129 | 1936 |

# Introduction – The 5XPs

When I commenced my apprenticeship at Crewe North, I already knew what my new-found colleagues meant when they referred to a "Black Un", as I was a life-long railway enthusiast. Not so, many of the other sobriquets bestowed on almost everything though, and it was perhaps doubly difficult for me, because of the somewhat different culture that was apparent between my native North Staffordshire and South Cheshire, despite the Potteries being separated from Crewe by but a few miles.

Railwaymen are of course renowned for their use of colloquialisms, and Crewe men were no exception. So, as I grappled with all sorts of new terminology, some obvious, others not, and although I knew what a "Black Un" was, I became mystified as to what was meant by a "Red Un". I reasoned that if a "Black Un" referred to an engine painted black, then a "Red Un" must refer to one painted red, and only a few of the 'Pacifics' were thus adorned, but surely they must be what was referred to as "Big Uns"! Indeed, there seemed to me to be nothing bigger – but then we had a Middle Shed, which was not in the middle of anywhere, so nothing would have surprised me. Eventually however, I elucidated that what I called a 'Jubilee', many Crewe men knew as a "Red Un"; decked out in LMS maroon when new, but otherwise externally similar to the Class 5, "Black Uns" so "Red Uns" they became then, and to some at least, that is what they had remained.

Actually, most people used the code 5X to describe them, and I never did hear a Crewe railwayman refer to the engines by their 'official' class name of 'Jubilee'. We had quite a number of them at Crewe North when I started work, 20 according to my notes, including all the early members of the class, Nos 5552-5556 inclusive, which, except for No. 5552, were the first batch built at Crewe in 1934. No. 5552 *Silver Jubilee* herself, had been the subject of one of those LMS "change of identity tricks", and had in fact, been built the following year, one of a later batch also built at Crewe, but originally starting life as No. 5642, the swap taking place in April 1935. This allowed a new locomotive, named *Silver Jubilee*, to be specially decked out in black livery, with a chrome-plated 'silver lining' effect, as part of the LMS celebrations for the Silver Jubilee of King George V and Queen Mary in that year.

The first engine of the type I actually worked on was No. 5631 *Tanganyika*, a long standing Crewe North allocated member of the class, and but the eleventh locomotive that was privileged to be maintained by my fair hands! She was undergoing a No. 8 Valve & Piston examination, on No. 6 road of the Middle Shed at Crewe North, and I helped remove, service, and refit her piston valves.

In my train spotting days, to all intents and purposes the class was split into three, those allocated to the former LNWR and Caledonian sheds, and which were all regular performers through Crewe, those at the old Midland and Glasgow & South Western depots, which one went to Derby to see, and lastly, those at the former Lancashire & Yorkshire Railway sheds, which were far more elusive from a Stoke-on-Trent base. The class was indeed spread far and wide, and there were thus great gaps in my *ABCs*, with some members allocated to North Eastern and Western Region sheds, the former in the West Riding of Yorkshire, and the latter at Bristol.

It has to be said that the 5Xs were one of the least successful of Stanier's designs, especially when new with their low degree of superheat, and early performances were very mediocre. Actually, among their first duties were the Euston to Birmingham and Wolverhampton two-hour expresses, and the aged 'Claughtons' were able to knock spots off them! In hindsight, it has been generally accepted that the added complication of the third cylinder was really unnecessary, but then their contemporary two-cylinder counterparts were so successful first time, and hindsight, unlike foresight, is an exact science! Most enginemen reckoned anything that they could get out of a 5XP, they could equal with a "Black Un" in good nick. Nevertheless, they did tend to get diagrammed for the harder and faster turns, but it was only after they had all received 24-element superheaters, and the men had grown accustomed to their more demanding foibles, that a consistent level of performance was achieved. However, they remained for all their lives somewhat temperamental machines, and always needed just that extra bit of effort, knowledge, experience, and not least skill, to get the best out of them, otherwise they were liable to deliver substandard performances, especially if everything was not 'just right'.

Perhaps the most outward difference in the appearance of the several variations among the class, (apart that is, from the two rebuilt as Class 7s, of which more anon), were their tenders. Most were paired with one or other of the Stanier 'standard' designs, 3,500 or 4,000 gallon capacity, but others had the much smaller, lower and narrower Fowler design. To my mind these never seemed to suit them, giving the whole ensemble a foreshortened effect. I particularly remember No. 5704 *Leviathan*, having this latter type of tender, because it was the only one at Crewe as far as I can recall, and moreover, one of very few so fitted, seen regularly on the West Coast Main Line. This machine, was Leviathan in name alone, and came to Crewe North from, I think, Edge Hill, around the turn of the years 1962-3. For many years prior to this it had been a Scottish Region engine, allocated to Carlisle Kingmoor, when that shed had come under that region's auspices. What a rattle trap it was, battered and bruised, and if the crews were to be believed, this was exactly what it did to them too. In awful condition, I know not when it had last been 'shopped', let alone painted, but try as we might, we could hardly get any green paint to show anywhere except on the tender sides. Nobody had a good word for her, and despite a lot of time and effort, we seemed unable to lift her reputation among those who had to drive and fire the locomotive. We were only too glad then, to see it despatched on transfer to Willesden (of all places) in January 1964, after a drop off in work at Crewe, following the Christmas rush – not that No. 5704 would have been any use at all, in any sort of rush!

Imagine our surprise then, when Willesden closed its doors to steam on 1st September 1964, for among the engines transferred to Crewe North was – yes, you have guessed it – 5704. Well we did not know what Willesden had been doing with old *Leviathan*, but one thing was certain, they had effected no improvement, and it continued to stagger about on local trips, blowing steam all over the place, shaking everything loose, and generally causing anybody and everybody who came into contact with her, a lot of heartache! Mercifully, orders came one day to place the locomotive in store, and this we were glad to do in the autumn of 1964. Actually, I see from my notes this took place on 26th October. It never steamed again after that, and was withdrawn the following January. Incidentally I notice, again from notes I took at the time, that all the remaining Crewe North allocated 5XPs were taken out of service that day, with Nos 5554, 5617 and 5672 being placed in store, whilst Nos 5676 and 5733 were withdrawn. Of our other two, the doyen of the class, No. 5552 (actually built as No. 5642 remember), had been withdrawn a few weeks earlier on 20th September. The other, No. 5595, survived a while longer and was another long time Crewe North Shed resident, but was transferred to Llandudno Junction, also on 20th October. As events turned out, none of those placed into store that day were to steam again.

Ironically, we had only completed No. 8 Valve & Piston examinations on two of them a few weeks earlier, No. 5554 on 1st September, and No. 5552 on 11th September, this was the largest shed examination we did. The latter engine only worked a matter of half a dozen days afterwards.

No less than 191 'Jubilees' were built, No. 5637 was scrapped following damage sustained in the Harrow accident of 1952, and Nos 5735 and 5736 were rebuilt as Class 7 engines, along the lines of the rebuilt 'Royal Scots', in 1943. This left 188 of the 'standard' engines, albeit with numerous minor differences, the majority of which would go unnoticed by most observers. The most notable of these was, as I have already mentioned, the tenders, although double chimneys did appear from time to time on several locomotives. All members of the class were decked out in BR green livery latterly, and as we have seen they were spread far and wide. What then should posterity record about them? That they saved tremendously on repair costs and increased availability over the types they replaced cannot be doubted, and their arrival sent scores of 'Claughtons' and their ilk to the scrap heap. But whether their maintenance costs in turn, so much higher than the Class 5 with its simple two-cylinder arrangement, were justified, is another story, and I fancy that the LMS and later BR, would have been better off financially, and little worse in performance terms, if 191 more Class 5s had been built instead.

However, visually they were far more attractive than the "Black Fives", in their original maroon and later green liveries and with names – an obvious attraction for the enthusiast fraternity, their syncopated three-cylinder rhythm making a grand sound too. In *The Power of the Jubilees* Gavin Morrison and John Whiteley have portrayed the locomotives during all their trials and tribulations, and in all their vicissitudes, not least where their finest performances were achieved, climbing the fells at Grayrigg, Shap or Blea Moor; and what a magnificent sight they make. I have enjoyed penning these few words, as I always do with these introductions for my friends' books. They give me an all too infrequent opportunity to dig out my old notebooks, and recall some happy and interesting times. I wish the book well, and if it finds readers who get half as much enjoyment as the authors and I have had in compiling it, then I know that Gavin and John will feel their efforts have been worthwhile.

Allan Baker

A pre-war picture of the cylinder and crosshead of a 'Jubilee', showing the vacuum pump from the left-hand crosshead. The pumps were only used until the beginning of the Second World War.
*C. R. L. Coles*

## The 5XP 'Jubilee' Class 4-6-0s

| LMS No. | Name(s) | Date introduced | Fitted with replacement domed boiler (1) | Withdrawn | LMS No. | Name(s) | Date introduced | Fitted with replacement domed boiler (1) | Withdrawn |
|---|---|---|---|---|---|---|---|---|---|
| 5552 | Silver Jubilee | 12/34 (2) | 9/40 | 9/64 | 5571 | South Africa | 9/34 | 5/38 | 5/56 |
| 5553 | Canada | 6/34 | 2/37 | 11/64 | 5572 | Irish Free State/Eire (9/38) | 9/34 | 5/37 | 1/64 |
| 5554 | Ontario | 6/34 | 6/36 | 11/64 | 5573 | Newfoundland | 9/34 | 3/38 | 9/65 |
| 5555 | Quebec | 6/34 | 10/38 | 8/63 | 5574 | India | 9/34 | 11/37 | 3/66 |
| 5556 | Nova Scotia | 6/34 | 2/37 | 9/64 | 5575 | Madras | 9/34 | 12/37 | 6/63 |
| 5557 | New Brunswick | 6/34 | 2/37 | 9/64 | 5576 | Bombay | 9/34 | 6/41 | 12/62 |
| 5558 | Manitoba | 7/34 | 11/37 | 8/64 | 5577 | Bengal | 9/34 | 7/39 | 9/64 |
| 5559 | British Columbia | 7/34 | 10/37 | 10/62 | 5578 | United Provinces | 9/34 | 4/38 | 5/64 |
| 5560 | Prince Edward Island | 7/34 | 6/37 | 11/63 | 5579 | Punjab | 10/34 | 5/38 | 8/64 |
| 5561 | Saskatchewan | 7/34 | 2/38 | 9/64 | 5580 | Burma | 10/34 | 6/37 | 12/64 |
| 5562 | Alberta | 8/34 | 6/37 | 11/67 | 5581 | Bihar and Orissa | 10/34 | 4/43 | 8/66 |
| 5563 | Australia | 8/34 | 1/39 | 11/65 | 5582 | Central Provinces | 11/34 | 11/37 | 12/62 |
| 5564 | New South Wales | 8/34 | 7/37 | 7/64 | 5583 | Assam | 11/34 | 1/38 | 10/64 |
| 5565 | Victoria | 8/34 | 6/37 | 1/67 | 5584 | North West Frontier | 12/34 | 8/38 | 9/64 |
| 5566 | Queensland | 8/34 | 3/37 | 11/62 | 5585 | Hyderabad | 12/34 | 6/37 | 5/64 |
| 5567 | South Australia | 8/34 | 4/37 | 1/65 | 5586 | Mysore | 12/34 | 2/37 | 1/65 |
| 5568 | Western Australia | 8/34 | 6/37 | 4/64 | 5587 | Baroda | 12/34 | 3/37 | 12/62 |
| 5569 | Tasmania | 8/34 | 6/37 | 4/64 | 5588 | Kashmir | 12/34 | 6/37 | 4/65 |
| 5570 | New Zealand | 8/34 | 8/37 | 12/62 | 5589 | Gwalior | 12/34 | 10/37 | 3/65 |

| LMS No. | Name(s) | Date introduced | Fitted with replacement domed boiler (1) | Withdrawn |
|---|---|---|---|---|
| 5590 | Travancore | 12/34 | 4/37 | 12/65 |
| 5591 | Udaipur | 12/34 | 6/38 | 10/63 |
| 5592 | Indore | 12/34 | 5/37 | 9/64 |
| 5593 | Kolhapur (3) | 12/34 | 4/37 | 10/67 |
| 5594 | Bhopal | 1/35 | 1/38 | 12/62 |
| 5595 | Southern Rhodesia | 1/35 | 3/37 | 1/65 |
| 5596 | Bahamas (3) | 1/35 | 11/37 | 7/66 |
| 5597 | Barbados | 1/35 | 2/38 | 1/65 |
| 5598 | Basutoland | 2/35 | 6/37 | 10/64 |
| 5599 | Bechuanaland | 1/35 | 8/37 | 8/64 |
| 5600 | Bermuda | 2/35 | 2/38 | 12/65 |
| 5601 | British Guiana | 4/35 | 9/37 | 9/64 |
| 5602 | British Honduras | 4/35 | 4/37 | 3/65 |
| 5603 | Solomon Islands | 3/35 | 10/37 | 12/62 |
| 5604 | Ceylon | 3/35 | 7/37 | 7/65 |
| 5605 | Cyprus | 4/35 | 4/38 | 2/64 |
| 5606 | Falkland Islands | 4/35 | 2/38 | 6/64 |
| 5607 | Fiji | 6/34 | 6/36 | 11/62 |
| 5608 | Gibraltar | 7/34 | 4/37 | 9/65 |
| 5609 | Gilbert and Ellice Islands | 7/34 | 9/38 | 9/60 |
| 5610 | Gold Coast/Ghana (12/58) | 7/34 | 2/37 | 1/64 |
| 5611 | Hong Kong | 7/34 | 8/38 | 9/64 |
| 5612 | Jamaica | 8/34 | 4/37 | 3/64 |
| 5613 | Kenya | 8/34 | 11/38 | 9/64 |
| 5614 | Leeward Islands | 8/34 | 12/36 | 1/64 |
| 5615 | Malay States | 8/34 | 2/37 | 12/62 |
| 5616 | Malta/Malta G. C. (11/43) | 8/34 | 7/36 | 1/61 |
| 5617 | Mauritius | 9/34 | 12/37 | 11/64 |
| 5618 | New Hebrides | 10/34 | 4/37 | 2/64 |
| 5619 | Nigeria | 10/34 | 3/37 | 8/61 |
| 5620 | North Borneo | 10/34 | 3/37 | 9/64 |
| 5621 | Northern Rhodesia | 10/34 | 6/37 | 12/62 |
| 5622 | Nyasaland | 10/34 | 7/36 | 9/64 |
| 5623 | Palestine | 10/34 | 8/39 | 7/64 |
| 5624 | St Helena | 10/34 | 12/38 | 11/63 |
| 5625 | Sarawak | 10/34 | 1/39 | 9/63 |
| 5626 | Seychelles | 11/34 | 2/37 | 10/65 |
| 5627 | Sierra Leone | 11/34 | 10/38 | 9/66 |
| 5628 | Somaliland | 11/34 | 2/37 | 12/62 |
| 5629 | Straits Settlements | 11/34 | 4/39 | 4/65 |
| 5630 | Swaziland | 11/34 | 11/38 | 11/61 |
| 5631 | Tanganyika | 11/34 | 12/38 | 8/64 |
| 5632 | Tonga | 11/34 | 8/38 | 10/65 |
| 5633 | Trans-Jordan/Aden (9/46) | 11/34 | 10/39 | 10/65 |
| 5634 | Trinidad | 11/34 | 4/39 | 5/63 |
| 5635 | Tobago | 11/34 | 3/39 | 9/64 |
| 5636 | Uganda | 12/34 | 3/37 | 12/62 |
| 5637 | Windward Islands | 12/34 | 10/38 | 12/52 |
| 5638 | Zanzibar | 12/34 | 11/36 | 3/64 |
| 5639 | Raleigh | 12/34 | 3/37 | 9/63 |
| 5640 | Frobisher | 12/34 | 8/36 | 3/64 |
| 5641 | Sandwich | 12/34 | 4/37 | 9/64 |
| 5642 | Boscawen | 5/34 (2) | 12/39 | 1/65 |
| 5643 | Rodney | 12/34 | 6/44 | 1/66 |
| 5644 | Howe | 12/34 | 10/38 | 11/63 |
| 5645 | Collingwood | 12/34 | 9/37 | 10/63 |
| 5646 | Napier | 12/34 | 3/38 | 12/63 |
| 5647 | Sturdee | 1/35 | 1/38 | 4/67 |
| 5648 | Wemyss | 1/35 | 12/37 | 2/63 |
| 5649 | Hawkins | 1/35 | 4/37 | 10/63 |
| 5650 | Blake | 1/35 | 1/37 | 1/63 |
| 5651 | Shovell | 1/35 | 1/37 | 1/63 |
| 5652 | Hawke | 1/35 | 5/37 | 1/65 |
| 5653 | Barham | 1/35 | 1/38 | 3/65 |
| 5654 | Hood | 2/35 | 5/37 | 6/66 |
| 5655 | Keith | 12/34 | 5/37 | 4/65 |
| 5656 | Cochrane | 12/34 | 3/37 | 12/62 |
| 5657 | Tyrwhitt | 12/34 | 4/37 | 9/64 |
| 5658 | Keyes | 12/34 | 6/37 | 9/65 |
| 5659 | Drake | 12/34 | 5/37 | 5/63 |
| 5660 | Rooke | 12/34 | 7/37 | 6/66 |
| 5661 | Vernon | 12/34 | 1/38 | 5/65 |
| 5662 | Kempenfelt | 12/34 | 7/38 | 11/62 |
| 5663 | Jervis | 1/35 | 7/38 | 10/64 |
| 5664 | Nelson | 1/35 | 4/37 | 5/65 |
| 5665 | Lord Rutherford of Nelson | 11/35 | | 12/62 |
| 5666 | Cornwallis | 11/35 | | 4/65 |
| 5667 | Jellicoe | 11/35 | | 1/65 |
| 5668 | Madden | 12/35 | | 12/63 |

| LMS No. | Name(s) | Date introduced | Fitted with replacement domed boiler (1) | Withdrawn |
|---|---|---|---|---|
| 5669 | Fisher | 12/35 | | 5/63 |
| 5670 | Howard of Effingham | 12/35 | | 10/64 |
| 5671 | Prince Rupert | 12/35 | | 11/63 |
| 5672 | Anson | 12/35 | | 11/64 |
| 5673 | Keppel | 12/35 | | 12/62 |
| 5674 | Duncan | 12/35 | | 10/64 |
| 5675 | Hardy | 12/35 | | 6/67 |
| 5676 | Codrington | 12/35 | | 9/64 |
| 5677 | Beatty | 12/35 | | 12/62 |
| 5678 | De Robeck | 12/35 | | 12/62 |
| 5679 | Armada | 12/35 | | 12/62 |
| 5680 | Camperdown | 12/35 | | 1/63 |
| 5681 | Aboukir | 12/35 | | 9/64 |
| 5682 | Trafalgar | 1/36 | | 6/64 |
| 5683 | Hogue | 1/36 | | 12/62 |
| 5684 | Jutland | 2/36 | | 12/65 |
| 5685 | Barfleur | 2/36 | | 4/64 |
| 5686 | St. Vincent | 2/36 | | 11/62 |
| 5687 | Neptune | 2/36 | | 12/62 |
| 5688 | Polyphemus | 2/36 | | 12/62 |
| 5689 | Ajax | 2/36 | | 12/64 |
| 5690 | Leander (3) | 3/36 | | 3/64 |
| 5691 | Orion | 3/36 | | 12/62 |
| 5692 | Cyclops | 3/36 | | 12/62 |
| 5693 | Agamemnon | 3/36 | | 12/62 |
| 5694 | Bellerophon | 3/36 | | 1/67 |
| 5695 | Minotaur | 3/36 | | 1/64 |
| 5696 | Arethusa | 4/36 | | 7/64 |
| 5697 | Achilles | 4/36 | | 9/67 |
| 5698 | Mars | 4/36 | | 10/65 |
| 5699 | Galatea (3) | 4/36 | | 11/64 |
| 5700 | Britannia/Amethyst (9/51) | 4/36 | | 7/64 |
| 5701 | Conqueror | 4/36 | | 2/63 |
| 5702 | Colossus | 5/36 | | 4/63 |
| 5703 | Thunderer | 5/36 | | 11/64 |
| 5704 | Leviathan | 5/36 | | 1/65 |
| 5705 | Seahorse | 5/36 | | 11/65 |
| 5706 | Express | 5/36 | | 9/63 |
| 5707 | Valiant | 5/36 | | 12/62 |
| 5708 | Resolution | 6/36 | | 2/64 |
| 5709 | Implacable | 6/36 | | 11/63 |
| 5710 | Irresistible | 6/36 | | 6/64 |
| 5711 | Courageous | 6/36 | | 12/62 |
| 5712 | Victory | 6/36 | | 11/63 |
| 5713 | Renown | 7/36 | | 10/62 |
| 5714 | Revenge | 7/36 | | 7/63 |
| 5715 | Invincible | 7/36 | | 12/62 |
| 5716 | Swiftsure | 7/36 | | 9/64 |
| 5717 | Dauntless | 7/36 | | 10/63 |
| 5718 | Dreadnought | 8/36 | | 10/62 |
| 5719 | Glorious | 8/36 | | 3/63 |
| 5720 | Indomitable | 8/36 | | 12/62 |
| 5721 | Impregnable | 8/36 | | 10/65 |
| 5722 | Defence | 8/36 | | 11/62 |
| 5723 | Fearless | 8/36 | | 8/64 |
| 5724 | Warspite | 9/36 | | 10/62 |
| 5725 | Repulse | 9/36 | | 12/62 |
| 5726 | Vindictive | 10/36 | | 3/65 |
| 5727 | Inflexible | 10/36 | | 12/62 |
| 5728 | Defiance | 10/36 | | 10/62 |
| 5729 | Furious | 10/36 | | 10/62 |
| 5730 | Ocean | 10/36 | | 10/63 |
| 5731 | Perseverance | 10/36 | | 10/62 |
| 5732 | Sanspareil | 10/36 | | 2/64 |
| 5733 | Novelty | 11/36 | | 9/64 |
| 5734 | Meteor | 11/36 | | 12/63 |
| 5735 | Comet | 11/36 | | 10/64 |
| 5736 | Phoenix | 11/36 | | 9/64 |
| 5737 | Atlas | 11/36 | | 5/64 |
| 5738 | Samson | 12/36 | | 12/63 |
| 5739 | Ulster | 12/36 | | 1/67 |
| 5740 | Munster | 12/36 | | 10/63 |
| 5741 | Leinster | 12/36 | | 1/64 |
| 5742 | Connaught | 12/36 | | 5/65 |

Notes

1.) Nos 5665-5742 were fitted with domed boilers from new.
2.) 5552 and 5642 swopped identities permanently in April 1935.
3.) Preserved.

*Above and Right* The locomotive shown in this series of pictures was in fact the second No. 5552, which was originally No. 5642, the locomotives changing identities to mark the Silver Jubilee of King George V in April 1935 as already noted. The original No. 5552 entered traffic in May 1934, whereas No. 5642 entered traffic in December 1934. The new No. 5552 was given a special livery of high gloss black, with plated raised cabside numbers and nameplate, which it retained until withdrawal in September 1964. These two pictures were taken when the locomotive was in British Railways lined green livery in the latter 1950s.

*Brian Morrison/Gavin Morrison*

*Below* The locomotive looked extremely smart in its special black livery. It is seen in this picture heading a 'down' Euston – Blackpool express at Hatch End in 1936. Note the highly polished buffers and chrome fittings which included the top feed cover, the steam pipes, boiler bands and hand rails.

*C. R. L. Coles*

## No. 5552 Silver Jubilee

*Above* An unusual location for No. 45552 *Silver Jubilee* on 27th June 1960 was Halifax Town station, when it was heading a parcels train. As can be seen from the shed plate, 8A, the locomotive was allocated to Edge Hill, Liverpool, at this time.

*Gavin Morrison*

*Below* A lucky picture taken at Oxenholme on 5th September 1952, shows No. 45552 *Silver Jubilee* heading a 'down' freight, as rebuilt 'Patriot' class 4-6-0 No. 45528 (then un-named) leaves on the 'up' 8.20am Carlisle – Euston.

*J. P. Wilson*

# Examples of the Different Batches

*Above* The first locomotive of the class, No. 5552 emerged from Crewe Works in April 1934, and was un-named. There were only five locomotives in the initial order, and the cost for locomotive and tender was authorised at £5,700 each. All five were completed by the end of June 1934. The first five locomotives originally had low superheat, domeless taper-boilers with vertical-throatplates, but these were replaced with a domed version by 1940. No. 5554 *Ontario* was photographed at Rugby shed on 24th July 1937, when fitted with one of the 3,500 gallon tenders which had $5\frac{1}{2}$ tons of coal capacity.

*J. M. Jarvis*

*Below* Twenty years separate this picture from the one above. No. 45554 *Ontario* in immaculate British Railways lined green livery is now running with a Stanier 4,000 gallon tender with 9 tons of coal capacity. The locomotive was allocated to Nottingham shed (16A) when this picture was taken and it is seen leaving Trent with an 'up' Manchester Central – St Pancras express on 13th March 1957.

*J. P. Wilson*

*Opposite top* No. 5556 *Nova Scotia*, originally built with a domeless boiler which was replaced with a domed version by February 1937. The locomotive is hauling a Camden – Walsall goods past Headstone Lane in 1939 when allocated to Willesden shed. Note that it is running with shorter than standard chimney.

*C. R. L. Coles*

*Opposite below* A most impressive picture of No. 45556 *Nova Scotia* working hard on an Easter relief from Euston to Workington, seen from a local train near Great Bridgeford north of Stafford in 1956. It was now running with the small 3,500 gallon tender that had replaced the Stanier 4,000 gallon version fitted in 1936, as seen above.

*M. Welch*

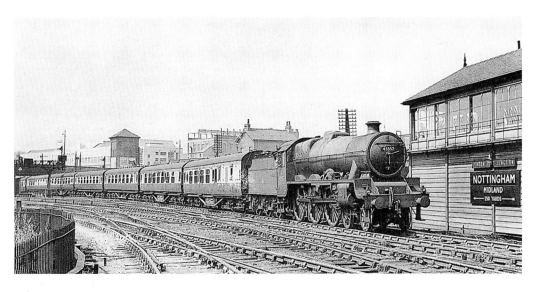

*Left* The batch of 50 locomotives commencing with No. 5557 *New Brunswick* was built by the North British Locomotive Company, 25 being constructed at the Hyde Park Works, and the other 25 at the Queen's Park site. Crewe continued construction after the completion of the first five, with another batch of 48 commencing with No. 5607. The LMS was desperate for the new locomotives, hence the reason for the North British Locomotive Co. getting involved. Delivery of the Scottish built locomotives was slower than anticipated, whereas Crewe Works, as usual, turned them out at a far faster rate, so the numerical order does not reflect the order they were completed and entered traffic. There were small variations between the Crewe and North British built locomotives, the Scottish locomotives having a 1½in longer wheelbase, although this became the standard length from No. 5655 onwards. No. 45557 *New Brunswick* passes London Road Junction at Nottingham with an 'up' Leeds express on 3rd August 1953.

*J. P. Wilson*

*Left* No. 45574, formerly *India*, is on Holbeck depot at Leeds on 28th June 1965. This was a Blackpool based locomotive for many years after the war, but finished its days at Leeds, and was withdrawn in March 1966. Note the yellow stripe on the cabside, banning its use on the West Coast Main Line south of Crewe.

*Gavin Morrison*

*Left* No. 5587 *Baroda* delivered new in December 1934 from the Queen's Park Works of the North British Locomotive Co., and running with a 3,500 gallon tender and shorter than standard chimney, passes Trent Junction on 4th June 1938, with an 'up' Manchester Central – St Pancras express.

*J. P. Wilson*

*Right* Another two North British built examples are seen on this page. No. 45603 *Solomon Islands* is heading a 'down' relief on the West Coast Main Line at Carpenders Park in July 1956.

*C. R. L. Coles*

*Below* No. 45604 *Ceylon* makes a spirited ascent of the 1 in 75 up Shap, and catches a glimpse of sunshine on a dismal day at Shap Wells, as it heads the 11.05am Birmingham – Edinburgh on 11th August 1959.

*R. H. Leslie*

*Above* The precise details of this picture are not known, but it is believed to be near Derby and probably taken just post war, judging by the position of the numbers, high on the cab side. No. 5612 *Jamaica* was the sixth in the second Crewe batch of 48 entering traffic in August 1934. It was running with one of the high-sided, narrow Fowler tenders, which were attached to many members of the class at different times.

F. G. Carrier

*Below* No. 45622 *Nyasaland* a Trafford Park, Manchester based locomotive for many years after the war, working an 'up' Manchester Central to St Pancras express at Long Eaton Junction on 19th April 1954. This second batch of 48 built by Crewe, each had a sanctioned cost of £6,600 – £900 more than the first five. It is interesting to note that the North British built examples, being constructed at the same time, were only sanctioned for £5,720 each. Although an extra £7,000 was subsequently added to the cost of the batch, the company suffered heavy losses through this order.

J. P. Wilson

*Above* This portrait of No. 5649, then un-named, was taken at Bedford shed in April 1936. Built at Crewe the locomotive entered traffic in January 1935 and is shown in original condition with a shorter than standard chimney. A domed boiler was fitted in April 1937.

*J. M. Jarvis*

*Below* No. 45647 *Sturdee* has been cleaned up ready to haul a Stephenson Locomotive Society special across the Pennines on 12th July 1964. It is seen here ready to leave Farnley Junction depot for Leeds City station.

*Gavin Morrison*

*Above* Only ten out of the total of 191 'Jubilees' were built at Derby Works in 1934/35, Nos 5655 – 5664. This pre-war picture shows No. 5657 *Tyrwhitt* storming past Edwalton at the head of an 'up' St Pancras express from Leeds on 24th March 1939. The locomotive was fitted with domed boiler in April 1937.

*J. P. Wilson*

*Below* No. 45660 *Rooke* finished its working days at Holbeck shed, Leeds, where it is seen under the coaler on 29th March 1965. This Derby built locomotive, with its 24-element superheater and vertical throatplate boiler, was used in October 1937 on dynamometer car trials between Bristol and Carlisle. With coal from Grimethorpe Colliery it achieved some of the highest recorded power outputs for the class.

*Gavin Morrison*

*Right* No. 45671 *Prince Rupert* was one of 17 of which were completed at Crewe in 1935. This batch of 30 altogether, were the first to be fitted with domed boilers with sloping throatplates from new. The locomotive is approaching Low Gill on 18th September 1962, leading a morning train from Crewe to Glasgow Central.

*Gavin Morrison*

*Below* No. 45680 *Camperdown* was another of the 1935/36 Crewe batch of 30. In 1958 it was photographed at the head of a Manchester London Road – Euston express on Moss Bank south of Macclesfield.

*M. Welch*

*Above* Construction of the 'Jubilees' was completed with No. 5742 in December 1936, Crewe Works producing the last 61 within the year. No. 45691 *Orion* works a 'down' parcels train up Shap Bank and is seen passing Scout Green on 30th June 1962.

*Gavin Morrison*

*Above* No. 45694 *Bellerophon* spent most of the post war years allocated to Holbeck depot, until being transferred to Low Moor and Wakefield for a short period before withdrawal in January 1967. It has just arrived on Holbeck after working the 'down' "Thames-Clyde Express" from St Pancras on 16th May 1960.

*Gavin Morrison*

*Below* This fine picture of No. 5683 *Hague* in original condition was taken in 1938, as it headed a 'down' Manchester express at Tring.

*C. R. L. Coles*

*Above* The 'up' "Thames-Clyde Express" passes Rockcliffe on 16th January 1955, powered by No. 45720 *Indomitable* which is attached to a narrow 3,500 gallon Fowler tender.

*R. H. Leslie*

*Below* The extensive trackwork at Wortley Junction, Leeds in the 1960s is in sharp contrast to the rationalised layout of today. No. 45686 *St. Vincent* heads north on the 1.54pm from Leeds to Carnforth on 5th June 1962.

*Gavin Morrison*

*Above* Clearly showing the 22A Bristol Barrow Road shed code, No. 45682 *Trafalgar* makes a vigorous departure from Bristol Temple Meads on an express for York in July 1953.

*C. R. L. Coles*

*Above* On 3rd September 1951, No. 45703 *Thunderer* passes Rugby at the head of what was probably an express from Birmingham, as the locomotive was allocated to Bushbury depot at the time.

*J. B. C. McCann*

*Below* No. 45697 *Achilles* was one of the last 'Jubilees' to be withdrawn, surviving at Holbeck depot until September 1967, being outlived only by Nos 45562 and 45593 in the following two months. This locomotive, based at Kingmoor for many years after the war, arrived at Holbeck around 1964 with a small Fowler tender, which was quickly exchanged for one of 4,000 gallon Stanier design. Carrying out one of the many railtour duties for the remaining Holbeck locomotives in 1965, 1966 and 1967, it is seen passing Bell Busk signal box on 11th December 1965, with a Warwickshire Railway Society special over the Settle-Carlisle line.

*Gavin Morrison*

*Right* A close up view of No. 45737 *Atlas* of Bushbury, seen at Euston in 1958, ready to leave on what was probably a Birmingham express.

*M. Welch*

*Middle Right* Farnley Junction, Leeds, 'Jubilee' No. 45695 *Minotaur* passes Bradley Junction on the outskirts of Huddersfield with the 4pm Hull-Liverpool Lime Street express on 27th August 1959.

*Gavin Morrison*

*Below* In terrible external condition, No. 45715 *Invincible* prepares to leave Holbeck depot to work the 'down' "Waverley" express to Carlisle on 21st September 1960. Based at Carlisle Kingmoor for many years, it retained the 3,500 gallon Fowler tender until withdrawn in December 1962.

*Gavin Morrison*

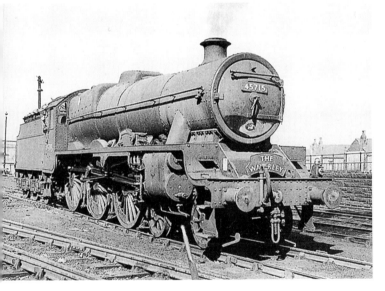

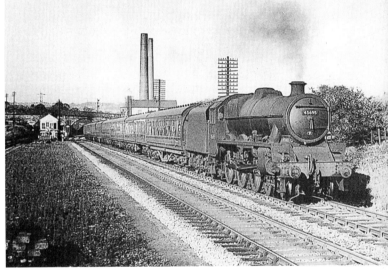

*Right* The final member of the class, No. 45742 *Connaught*, photographed on Holbeck depot, Leeds on 31st May 1963. Built in December 1936 at Crewe, it was withdrawn in May 1965. Between 1946 and 1949 it was fitted with a 2B domed and 28-element superheater boiler and also a double chimney from 1940 until November 1955. It was a Bushbury locomotive for many years and performed regularly on the 2-hour Birmingham – Euston expresses.

*Gavin Morrison*

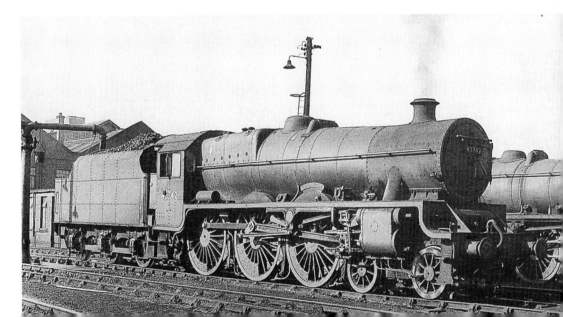

# Liveries

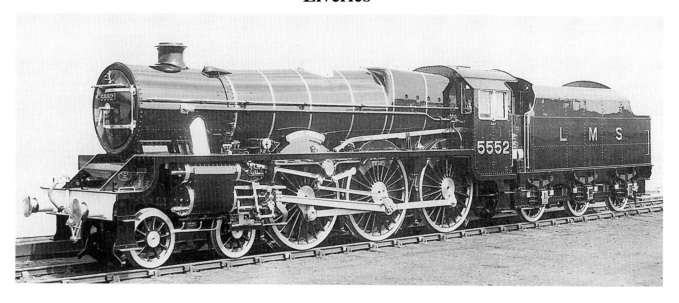

*Above* As already illustrated on pages 1, 6 and 7, No. 5552 (originally No. 5642) was given a special livery of high-gloss black with chromium embellishments and named *Silver Jubilee* in honour of the 25 years reign of King George V. It first appeared with its name at an exhibition of rolling stock on 2nd and 3rd May 1935. This livery lasted on the locomotive through the war years until mid-1945 when the chrome numerals were painted white for a while, but the black base colour carried on until the 1950s when it received BR lined green. Fifteen years without re-painting speaks well for the original black paint finish.

*National Railway Museum*

*Below* A superb study of No. 5620, later named *North Borneo* at the head of a 'down' express at St Pancras in 1936. It is resplendent in the original red livery with the large scroll and serif insignia. The first 113 locomotives entered service without being named. Locomotive Nos 5721 to 5742 received sans serif type lettering when new, before the LMS reverted to the original painting style in 1938.

*C. R. L. Coles*

*Right* During the war years unlined black with unshaded yellow numbers was used, but in 1946 lined black was adopted by the LMS, as illustrated in this picture of No. 5648 *Wemyss* on a 'down' St Pancras – Manchester express passing Mill Hill in 1946.

C. R. L. Coles

*Below* Until the BR livery was finalised an 'M' prefix was added to the numbers of thirteen members of the class, and three other locomotives had "British Railways" lettering on the tender. An 'M' prefix was also added to some of the smokebox numbers. Many received the "British Railways" on the tender with 40,000 added to the number, as shown in this picture of 45686 *St. Vincent* taken in 1950 near Farrington.

W. H. Foster

*Above* Only a few locomotives received the lined black livery later adopted for the mixed traffic classes. No. 45695 *Minotaur* with small Fowler tender, works north on a Euston–Blackpool express on 1st June 1951 at Bushey & Oxhey.

*Brian Morrison*

*Below* Obviously just ex-works, No. 45678 *De Robeck*, having had the lined black livery treatment at Crewe Works, poses for the photographer at Rugby shed on 15th February 1949.

*J. M. Jarvis*

*Right* Before Nationalisation, around 1945, No. 5573 *Newfoundland* was given a blue-grey livery, lined in maroon and gilt, while No. 5594 *Bhopal* was the only locomotive to receive the crimson lake livery after the war, although ten managed to retain the red livery when the BR numbers were added. Locomotive Nos 45565, 45604 and 45694 were painted in light green livery, fully lined in red, grey and black, with pale straw insignia. No. 45565 *Victoria* in green livery is seen leaving St Pancras for Leeds in 1948.

C. R. L. Coles

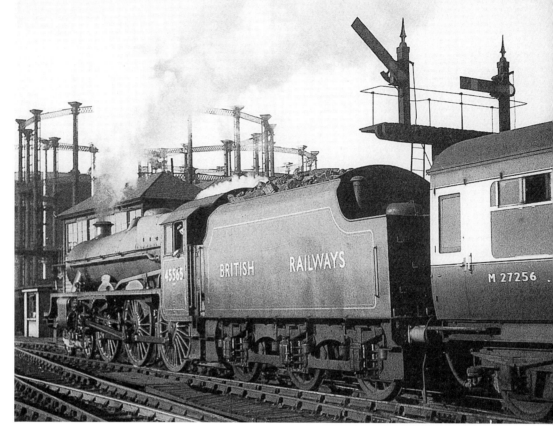

*Below* Another of the light green experimental livery locomotives, No. 45694 *Bellerophon* is seen at Nottingham Midland on a Leeds express, 8th June 1948.

J. P. Wilson

*Left* The livery finally chosen by British Railways for the class was GWR Brunswick green with black, orange and black lining, with sans serif numerals in off-white, and the lion and wheel emblem on the tender. No. 45636 *Uganda* in this livery enters Elstree Tunnel with a 'down' Nottingham express in June 1953.

*C. R. L. Coles*

*Right* Just ex-works on 19th June 1960, in the lined green livery, with the new tender emblem introduced in 1957, No. 45715 *Invincible* is on Carlisle Kingmoor depot with the 12 inch numerals used by St Rollox Works for Scottish-based locomotives. The locomotive only lasted 18 months after this overhaul.

*Gavin Morrison*

*Left* No. 45695 *Minotaur* in the lined green livery is on Farnley Junction depot, Leeds on 7th June 1961.

*Gavin Morrison*

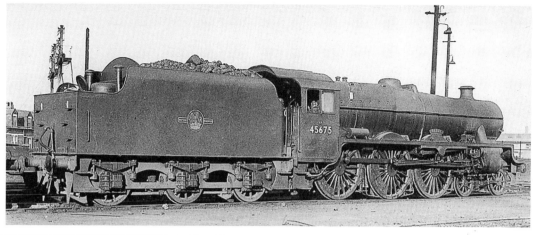

*Right* The last locomotives overhauled at Crewe received an unlined green livery as shown in this picture of No. 45675 *Hardy* on Holbeck depot, Leeds on 25th August 1964.

*Gavin Morrison*

*Left* No. 45562 *Alberta* at Carlisle Kingmoor depot shows the diagonal yellow cabside stripe, added in September 1964 to all members of the class, indicating they were banned from use on the electrified West Coast Main Line south of Crewe. By this date, 7th October 1967, it had lost its nameplates, and was attached to an unlined green tender.

*Gavin Morrison*

*Right* Unlined green with yellow stripe was the final livery for No. 45593 *Kolhapur*, seen without nameplates at Holbeck depot on 2nd June 1966.

*Gavin Morrison*

# Tenders

*Left* The class received four types of tender, and interchanging between locomotives occurred frequently. The Fowler 3,500 gallon tender with 5½ ton coal capacity, was originally fitted to new locomotives Nos 5552 – 5556. Nos 5695 – 5725 and 5740 had tenders of this type transferred from 'Royal Scots'. No. 45714 *Revenge* shows this 3,500 gallon, 5½ ton capacity example, as it simmers gently on Hellifield shed on 29th June 1961. The air breather pipes were in the coal space.

*Gavin Morrison*

*Below* Only ten Fowler modified tenders with high straight sides were built in 1934 and originally attached to locomotives Nos 5607–5616. They were interchanged freely amongst the class, and to other classes such as 'Patriots' and Midland 4F 0-6-0s in later years. No. 45719 *Glorious* of Bank Hall depot, Liverpool was running with one in the latter 1950s and was photographed at Carlisle Kingmoor shed on 30th August 1958.

*Gavin Morrison*

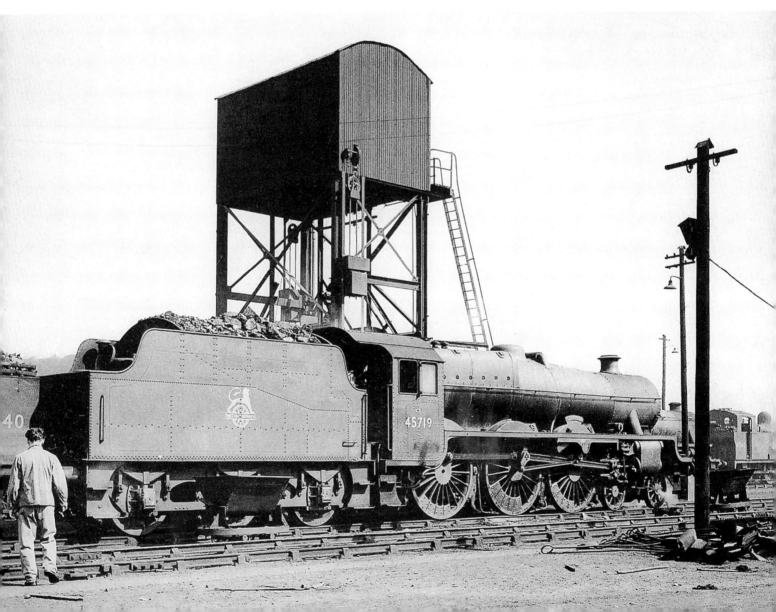

*Right* The differences between the 3,500 and 4,000 gallon versions of the Stanier tenders were not easy to identify, but No. 45593 *Kolhapur* finished its days attached to the 3,500 gallon, 7 ton coal capacity version, No. 4626 built in 1934, as shown in this photograph of it taking water on Holbeck depot, 15th July 1967.

*John Whiteley*

*Below* A 4,000 gallon, 9 ton tender is illustrated, attached to No. 45562 *Alberta*, of the flush welded type. The 'Jubilees' did not haul many Royal trains or similar workings during their careers, but amazingly on 30th May 1967, Holbeck turned out No. 45562 to take the Duke of Edinburgh down the Ripon line. It was photographed returning with the empty stock from Ripon at South Stainley. This is believed to have been the last steam working of the Royal Train on British Rail.

*Gavin Morrison*

# Developments and Modifications

*Above* From 1937 onwards four locomotives, Nos 5553, 5596, 5684 and 5742 were fitted with double chimneys, the first being No. 5684 *Jutland* when it was fitted with this Kylchap double blastpipe and chimney. This caused excessive spark-throwing and build-up of ash in the smokebox, so it only ran in this form for less than one year.

*National Railway Museum*

*Right* It was as late as 1956 before No. 45722 *Defence* was selected to visit the Rugby stationary test plant, with a view to improving steaming with poor quality coal. A double exhaust produced improved performance, but was removed in 1957. These two pictures show the locomotive at the test plant during trials in 1956. Various modifications as a result of these tests were made to eight locomotives with single chimneys, with No. 45596 *Bahamas* receiving a double blastpipe and chimney.

*J. B. C. McCann*

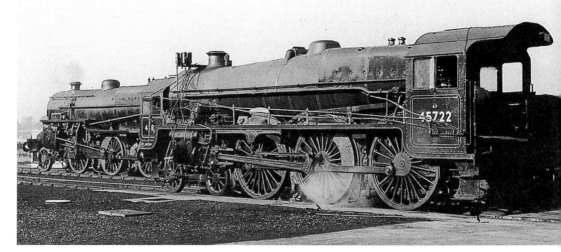

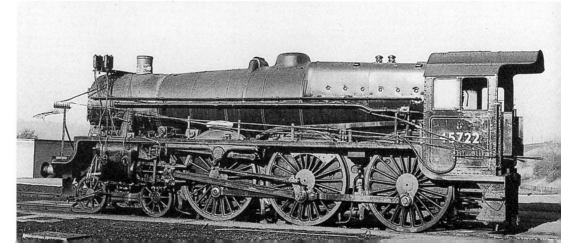

30

*Above* No. 45742 *Connaught* ran with a plain double exhaust chimney from 1940 to November 1955. It was surprising that no more were modified, as this locomotive could outperform the other members of the class on the Euston – Birmingham 2-hour expresses. This picture shows the locomotive south of Rugby on the 11.55am Wolverhampton – Euston in December 1952.

*J. B. C. McCann*

*Below* Another view of No. 45742 passing the impressive gantries at Heaton Norris near Stockport on a 'down' express around 1955.

*T. Lewis*

*Above* No. 45596 *Bahamas* was out-shopped from Crewe Works in 1961 fitted with a double blastpipe and chimney, which it retained until withdrawn and subsequently into preservation. The locomotive is based at Ingrow West on the Keighley & Worth Valley Railway and painted in BR lined green livery. It is seen here on Farnley Junction depot at Leeds on 5th September 1963, parted from its tender. after a minor collision with a Class 08 diesel shunter.

*Gavin Morrison*

*Below* Another view of No. 45596 *Bahamas*, now with a yellow stripe on the cabside, pulling out of Copley Hill sidings with a freight for Lancashire on 22nd April 1965.

*Gavin Morrison*

# The Rebuilt Locomotives

In the early 1940s the LMS was short of big express motive power, and in spite of all the modifications made to the steaming of the 'Jubilees', they were still short of expectations. In 1942 the decision was taken to rebuild two members of the class, Nos 5735 *Comet* and 5736 *Phoenix*. This was carried out in 1942 and the locomotives were fitted with entirely new 2A type boilers and new exhaust system, plus other modifications. They were used frequently on Leeds – Glasgow services, and Leeds – Bristol trains. Their performance was excellent, the Settle and Carlisle again proving a good testing route. As the Fowler 'Scots' were having trouble with leaky smokeboxes, they were chosen for rebuilding instead of further 'Jubilees', together with some of the 'Patriots', so only these two 'Jubilees' were converted. They were replaced at Leeds Holbeck by rebuilt 'Royal Scots' and transferred away to Camden depot where they spent many years working on the West Coast Main Line. Smoke deflectors were fitted in 1950, and they both survived until September/October 1964, No. 45736 being withdrawn from Carlisle Kingmoor.

*Above* No. 45736 *Phoenix* when based at Carlisle Kingmoor is on humble duties, ready to leave Bradford Forster Square on the 3.40pm all stations to Carlisle on 5th June 1964.
*Gavin Morrison*

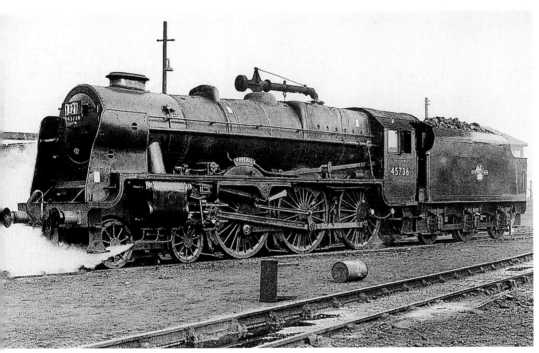

*Above and Right* Two pictures of a well cleaned No. 45736 *Phoenix* taken on Holbeck depot, Leeds, after it had worked a football special from Carlisle as far as Leeds. Another special on the same day was headed by rebuilt 'Patriot' No. 45527 *Southport*. Carlisle United usually did well in the FA Cup in the early 1960s, and the Carlisle depots nearly always cleaned the engines which were rostered to take the supporters to away matches. The date was 25th January 1964.

*Gavin Morrison*

*Left* A classic view of No. 45735 *Comet*, probably taken in the early 1950s, working a West Coast Main Line express.

*T. Lewis*

*Below* A superb study of No. 45736 *Phoenix* taken on 26th May 1953, as it leaves Kilsby Tunnel at the head of an 'up' Wolverhampton – Euston express.

*J. P. Wilson*

# At Work on the Titled Trains

*Right* Not long after the removal of its double chimney in November 1955, No. 45742 *Connaught* bursts from under the overbridge at Harrow & Wealdstone in July 1956, at the head of the 'down' "Midlander", one of the Euston – Birmingham 2-hour expresses.
*C. R. L. Coles*

*Below* Another view of the 'down' "Midlander", this time with one of the Bushbury depot stud of 'Jubilees', No. 45740 *Munster*, seen at Headstone Lane, and still fitted with 3,500 gallon Fowler tender in July 1954.
*C. R. L. Coles*

*No. 45595 Southern Rhodesia* blasts its way south, under the Northampton flyover at Rugby, running 80 minutes late due to an accident at Polesworth with the 'up' "Mancunian" on 19th November 1951. The tender is still lettered LMS.

*J. B. C. McCann*

The 'up' "Merseyside Express" was normally rostered for something larger than a 'Jubilee', but No. 45721 *Impregnable* is making a spirited departure from Rugby in January 1952. The locomotive is in lined black livery, with "British Railways" on the tender.

*J. B. C. McCann*

*Above* On the ash pits at Holbeck depot, No. 45699 *Galatea* of Barrow Road depot, Bristol is being serviced after working the 'down' "Devonian" on 17th May 1960. The locomotive is preserved but not currently in working order.

*Gavin Morrison*

*Above Right* A transport policewoman heads off down the platform at Leeds City after checking the validity of the photographer's permit before No. 45730 *Ocean* departs for Carlisle on the 'down' "Waverley" on 28th May 1960.

*Gavin Morrison*

*Right* Followers of preserved steam in the 1990s would find it hard to believe how dirty locomotives could be in the early 1960s. No. 45732 *Sanspareil* of Kingmoor depot, in terrible external condition, passes Marley Junction between Bingley and Keighley on the 'down' "Waverley" on 11th June 1960.

*Gavin Morrison*

*Above* Showing the large crest over the nameplate, No. 45595 *Southern Rhodesia* heads the 'down' "Comet" over the water troughs at Bushey in the early 1950s.

C. R. L. Coles

*Below* Journey's end for the 'up' "Mancunian", as No. 45638 *Zanzibar* stands at the buffer stops at Platform 6, Euston in 1958. This working was normally hauled by a rebuilt 'Royal Scot'.

M. Welch

*Below* The "Mancunian" departed at 9.45am from Manchester London Road for Euston. Again, 'Jubilee' hauled, No. 45718 *Dreadnought* storms through Watford cutting on 9th August 1952 with the 'up' working.

Brian Morrison

*Right* It was probably on the Midland main line that the 'Jubilees' put up their best performances as the trains tended to be lighter than the West Coast Main Line expresses, and therefore better suited to the locomotives. No. 45667 *Jellicoe*, a Nottingham based engine in 1959, makes a fine sight as it approaches Harlington station with the 'up' "Robin Hood".

M. Welch

*Below* Another view of the 'up' "Robin Hood", but this time headed by No. 45650 *Blake*, again in 1959, seen approaching Harlington.

M. Welch

# Around the Sheds

*Left* A scene that rather takes the glamour away from the steam engine, showing No. 45669 *Fisher* at Camden shed having the smokebox cleaned out under the coaler in May 1955. This picture really captures the atmosphere of the coaler/ashpit environment of the depot.

*C. R. L. Coles*

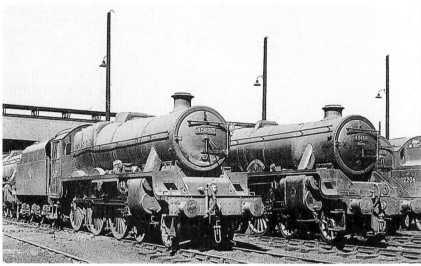

*Above* No. 45692 *Cyclops*, then allocated to Perth, is seen dead on Sunday 14th September 1959, at St Rollox, Glasgow, alongside one of the four named Stanier Class 5s, No. 45158 *Glasgow Yeomanry*, all of which were allocated to this depot at this time.

*Gavin Morrison*

*Below* On 29th June 1962, Carlisle Kingmoor based No. 45714 *Revenge* simmers gently on Hellifield shed, no doubt awaiting a duty to take it back to Carlisle over the Settle – Carlisle line. Note the large numbers, which were a feature of locomotives overhauled at St Rollox Works, Glasgow.

*Gavin Morrison*

*Right* The Midland shed at Bath has No. 45682 *Trafalgar* standing outside on 23rd April 1962. The locomotive was allocated to Bristol Barrow Road (82E) at the time. 'Jubilees' were frequent visitors to Bath Green Park with workings to and from the North, but they never worked south over the Somerset and Dorset line.

*Gavin Morrison*

*Below* Crewe North locomotive No. 45591 *Udaipur* is seen in the sunshine outside Shrewsbury shed on 21st July 1954. Standard Class 5 No. 73012 is in the background.

*Brian Morrison*

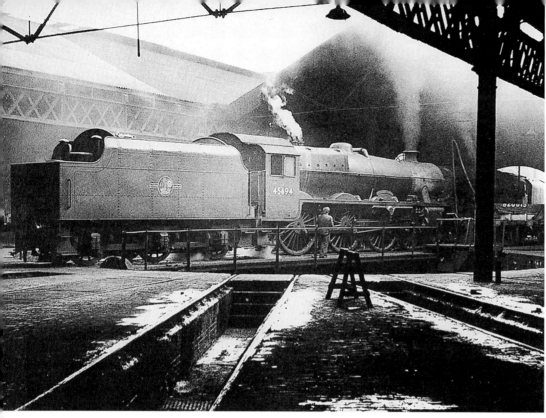

*Left* The gloomy interior of the roundhouse at Kentish Town (14B) shows Holbeck 'Jubilee' No. 45694 *Bellerophon* on the turntable in 1959.

*M. Welch*

*Below* Inside Holbeck shed on 30th April 1962, is Corkerhill (Glasgow) based locomotive No. 45727 *Inflexible*, withdrawn in December 1962, alongside No. 45675 *Hardy*, which was at its home shed.

*Gavin Morrison*

*Right* A Standard Class 9F 2-10-0 is alongside No. 45697 *Achilles* in Holbeck yard on 15th July 1967 with a Class 47 diesel behind. The picture shows well the unfavourable conditions under which the diesels were kept at steam depots.

*John Whiteley*

*Below* A study of No. 45593 *Kolhapur* also taken on 15th July 1967 inside Holbeck shed a few months before it closed to steam. The locomotive was kept well cleaned in 1966 and 1967 for rail tours and working Saturday extras north over the Settle – Carlisle line.

*John Whiteley*

*Below* The last three 'Jubilees' in service, together with a couple of Class 5s, lined up inside Holbeck depot on 1st July 1967. Obviously there was no work for them on this day. From the left is No. 45562 *Alberta*, an unidentified Class 5, No. 45697 *Achilles*, No. 45593 *Kolhapur* and Class 5 No. 45424.

*Gavin Morrison*

*Above* An interesting comparison of motive power taken at Carlisle Kingmoor shed on 30th August 1958, was Bank Hall (27A) locomotive No. 45719 *Glorious*, together with the Caledonian Single No. 123, which had been brought from St Rollox Works for an exhibition. London & North Western 2-4-0 No. 790 *Hardwicke* was also present.

*Gavin Morrison*

*Below* An unusual picture of No. 45596 *Bahamas* separated from its tender at Farnley Junction shed, Leeds. The locomotive had been in a minor collision with a Class 08 diesel shunter, the impact causing the tender body to become partly detached from the frame; no damage was apparently done to the 08! The ensemble had been assembled to be towed to Crewe Works, on 5th September 1963.

*Gavin Morrison*

# Re-Named Locomotives

*Left* A picture in Holbeck shed yard of No. 45610 *Ghana*, originally named *Gold Coast* until December 1958, alongside No. 45675 *Hardy*, on 31st May 1962.

*Gavin Morrison*

*Below* No. 45700 was originally named *Britannia* until September 1951, when it was changed to *Amethyst*. It was a Newton Heath locomotive when this picture was taken on 23rd March 1963, although it is shown at another Manchester shed, Trafford Park.

*Gavin Morrison*

*Right* The 1.54pm Leeds – Carnforth passes through the woods near Keighley golf course on 20th June 1962 headed by No. 45633 *Aden*, which until September 1946 was named *Trans-Jordan*.

*Gavin Morrison*

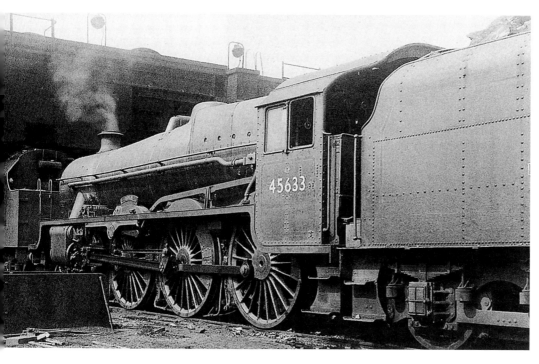

*Left* A close up of No. 45633, showing clearly the *Aden* nameplate, taken on Camden shed in August 1955.

*C. R. L. Coles*

*Right* No. 45572 *Eire* is shown entering Ashchurch on the 12.48pm York – Bristol on 2nd May 1959. Until September 1938 the locomotive was named *Irish Free State*. There is an interesting comparison to be made with the picture taken at the same location on Page 100.

*J. D. Edwards*

# The Midland Main Line

*Left* Kentish Town (14B) based locomotive No. 5614 *Leeward Islands* is ready to leave St Pancras with a 'down' express in 1937. It can just be seen that the locomotive is paired to one of the high sided, narrow Fowler tenders.

*F. G. Carrier*

*Below* Twenty-two years separate the picture above from this one at St Pancras, showing No. 45611 *Hong Kong* ready to leave with the 12.55pm express to Leicester on 31st August 1959.

*J. D. Edwards*

*Right* On Easter Saturday, 12th April 1952, the "Thames-Clyde Express" emerges from Elstree Tunnel, and approaches Elstree & Borehamwood station hauled by Holbeck locomotive No. 45568 *Western Australia.*
*Brian Morrison*

*Right* A 'down' Bradford Forster Square – St Pancras express approaches Elstree Tunnel in 1953 behind No. 45611 *Hong Kong.*
*C. R. L. Coles*

*Below* Another Holbeck based locomotive, No. 45569 *Tasmania,* heads a St Pancras – Bradford express near Mill Hill on 25th May 1957.
*Brian Morrison*

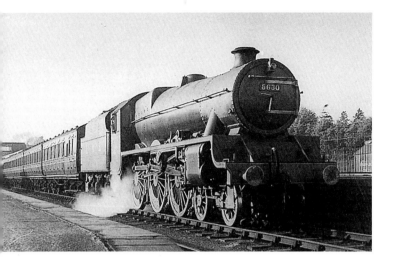

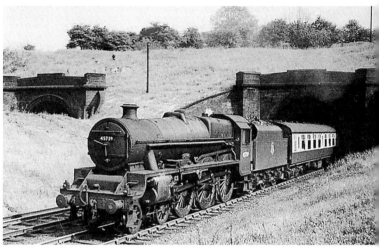

*Above* No. 5630, before being named *Swaziland*, and when only about six months old, pauses at Harpenden station on the 'up' slow line with a stopping train for St Pancras. The photographer's comment says that some of the low superheat locomotives were such poor performers in 1935 that they were given jobs normally carried out by the LMS Class 2, 3 or 4P 4-4-0s.

*J. M. Jarvis*

*Above* A 'down' St Pancras express appears from Elstree Tunnel in June 1955 with No. 45739 *Ulster* in charge.

*C. R. L. Coles*

*Below* No. 45641 *Sandwich* in full cry, storms up the bank to Ampthill Tunnel in 1959 with an 'up' Nottingham – St Pancras express.

*M. Welch*

*Below* A powerful picture of Sheffield Millhouses based locomotive, No. 45602 *British Honduras* near Ampthill Tunnel with an 'up' express from Sheffield to St Pancras in 1959.

*M. Welch*

*Right* No. 5725 *Repulse* approaches Kettering in 1938 at the head of a 'down' Bradford – St Pancras express.

C. R. L. Coles

*Below* With its 20A shed plate indicating it is allocated to Holbeck depot, No. 45608 *Gibraltar* bursts out of Elstree Tunnel into the May sunshine in 1952, with a 'down' St Pancras – Bradford express.

C. R. L. Coles

*Left* An 'up' Leeds City to St Pancras express passes London Road Junction Nottingham, with Holbeck 'Jubilee' No. 45597 *Barbados* in charge on 15th June 1950. The locomotive remained allocated to Holbeck until withdrawal in January 1965. It is painted in the smart lined black British Railways livery, later adopted for the mixed traffic locomotives, but with "British Railways" in full on the side of the 3,500 gallon tender. Only a few members of the class received this livery.

*J. P. Wilson*

*Left* An early post Nationalisation picture of No. 45659 *Drake*, still with the tender lettered "LMS". It is seen at the head of an 'up' Leeds City – St Pancras express passing Edwalton on 23rd October 1948.

*J. P. Wilson*

*Below* Several members of the class in the early 1950s were fitted with a standard BR chimney, instead of the usual Stanier pattern. No. 45629 *Straits Settlements* based at Trafford Park, Manchester, received one of these chimneys, and was photographed leaving Trent station on an 'up' Manchester Central – St Pancras working on 14th April 1952.

*J. P. Wilson*

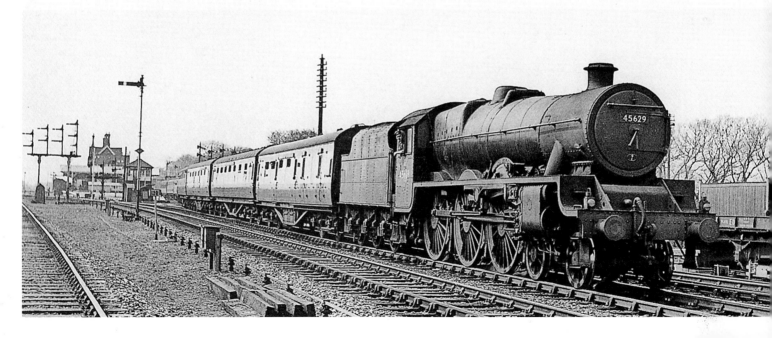

*Right* No. 45565 *Victoria* of Holbeck shed, was one of the three 'Jubilees' selected for experimental liveries following Nationalisation. When this picture was taken on 7th July 1948, it was painted in light green, fully lined out in red, grey and black with pale straw insignia. The train is a 'down' St Pancras – Leeds City express, and is near Lenton in Nottinghamshire.

*J. P. Wilson*

*Below* Another picture taken in the Nottingham area. This time it is of No. 45640 *Frobisher* on a 'down' Edinburgh train at West Bridgford, approaching Grantham Canal Bridge on 3rd August 1953.

*J. P. Wilson*

*Above* A fine picture of the now preserved No. 45690 *Leander* storming through Dore & Totley with an 'up' York – Bristol express in the early 1950s. This was another locomotive to receive the fully lined British Railways black livery, and was allocated to Bristol Barrow Road for many years after the war.

*B. R. Goodlad*

*Below* Running as British Railways No. 45696 *Arethusa* still has "LMS" painted on the tender, which suggests that the picture was taken around 1949 or 1950. The location is Romiley, and the train is probably a Manchester Central – Derby local.

*T. Lewis*

# At Work on the London & North Western Main Line

*Right* August 1963 sees No. 45726 *Vindictive* ready to depart from Euston with an express for Liverpool Lime Street. The locomotive was based at Crewe North at that time.

C. R. L. Coles

*Below* At the Euston buffer stops for Platforms 1 and 2 on 1st June 1951 after working expresses from Liverpool and Blackpool. This picture is of particular interest as the 'Jubilee' on the left is No. 45637 *Windward Islands*, which was one of the locomotives involved in the disastrous accident at Harrow & Wealdstone on 8th October 1952 and damaged beyond repair. As a result of this it is difficult to find photographs of the locomotive in working order. The Fowler 'Royal Scot' is No. 46134 *The Cheshire Regiment*.

Brian Morrison

*Above* No. 45601 *British Guiana* climbs Camden Bank from Euston on 7th October 1958 with a 'down' express.
British Railways Standard 2-6-4T No. 80068 is in the foreground with empty carriage stock for Camden yard.

*Brian Morrison*

*Right* Rebuilt 'Jubilee' No. 45735 *Comet* heads a 'down' express for Blackpool Central through Tring Cutting in April 1953.

C. R. L. Coles

*Below* Working a 'down' Northampton express No. 45721 *Impregnable* passes through Tring Cutting in May 1952.

C. R. L. Coles

*Above Right* Passing Hatch End in June 1953 is the 'down' "Midlander" headed by No. 45688 *Polyphemus*.

C. R. L. Coles

*Right* No. 45737 *Atlas*, on the 'up' "Midlander", the 11am from Wolverhampton High Level to Euston, picks up water from Bushey troughs on 25th March 1963.

Brian Morrison

*Above* A powerful picture of No. 45595 *Southern Rhodesia* in full forward gear at the head of an 'up' Manchester – Euston express at Cheddington in 1959.

*M. Welch*

*Below* A view of rebuilt 'Jubilee' No. 45736 *Phoenix* on an 'up' Halifax – Manchester – Euston express near Hillmorton, Rugby, on 11th December 1951.

*J. B. C. McCann*

*Above* No. 45709 *Implacable* of Bushbury shed nears Cheddington on an 'up' Wolverhampton High Level – Euston express in 1959.

*M. Welch* 59

*Left* Rebuilt No. 45736 *Phoenix* pauses at Stafford on 7th August 1956 at the head of a 'down' express from Euston to Holyhead.

*Brian Morrison*

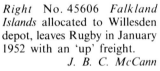

*Right* No. 45606 *Falkland Islands* allocated to Willesden depot, leaves Rugby in January 1952 with an 'up' freight.

*J. B. C. McCann*

*Left* Displaying an express headcode for this three-coach, 11.45am Liverpool – Rugby train, No. 45737 *Atlas* pauses at Atherstone on 28th May 1961 as it works south.

*Hugh Ballantyne*

*Above* A busy scene at Crewe from the famous footbridge at the north end of the station shows Nos 45698 *Mars* and 45688 *Polyphemus* on stock prior to heading north in 1959.

M. Welch

*Below* A Birmingham New Street – Manchester London Road express re-starts from Stafford on 7th August 1956 hauled by No. 45617 *Mauritius* and "Black 5" No. 44902.

Brian Morrison

*Left* A Saturday extra express approaches Acton Grange Junction near Warrington, near the bridge over the Manchester Ship Canal, in the pouring rain headed by No. 45556 *Nova Scotia* on 7th September 1963.
*Gavin Morrison*

*Left* Two very dirty locomotives Nos 45629 *Straits Settlements* and 45726 *Vindictive* leave Hest Bank on an 'up' Workington – Barrow – Euston express on 7th June 1960.
*Gavin Morrison*

*Below* A Locomotive Club of Great Britain special headed by Stockport based No. 45654 *Hood*, passes Grayrigg signal box on its journey north on 6th November 1965.
*Gavin Morrison*

*Right* After passing the summit at Grayrigg, No. 45649 *Hawkins* accelerates the morning Saturday's only Southport – Glasgow Central train round the "S" bend before Low Gill station and the Lune Gorge, on 1st September 1962.

*Gavin Morrison*

*Below* Recently allocated to Bank Hall depot (27A) at Liverpool, No. 45657 *Tyrwhitt* storms through the Lune Gorge to gain as much speed as possible in order to fill the tender on Dillcar troughs and for the climb to Shap Summit, with a Liverpool Exchange – Glasgow Central express on 18th August 1962.

*Gavin Morrison*

*Left* With only two months to go before withdrawal, No. 45736 *Phoenix* in poor external condition climbs past Shap Wells on a long van train, probably the 9.25am from Crewe on 26th July 1964.
*John Whiteley*

*Below* Another fine picture at the famous Shap Wells location, this time showing Kingmoor locomotive No. 45730 *Ocean* on 16th August 1958, at the head of the 2pm Manchester Victoria – Glasgow Central express.
*R. H. Leslie*

*Right* The hard shovelling is over for the fireman on No. 45578 *United Provinces* and Class 5 No. 45197 as they pass Shap Summit on 7th August 1961. The train is the 'up' morning Glasgow Central – Birmingham New Street express, normally a Stanier Pacific working.

*Gavin Morrison*

*Below* No. 45562 *Alberta* took the "South Yorkshireman" special from Bradford Exchange to Carlisle, on the outward journey via Shap and returning via the Settle and Carlisle line on 7th October 1967. The special is seen passing Shap Summit, on what must have been one of, if not the last, occasion a 'Jubilee' climbed Shap.

*John Whiteley*

*Left* Two pictures showing one of the famous post war trio of Bank Hall 'Jubilees', No. 45698 *Mars*, climbing to Shap Summit past Little Strickland with the 2pm Glasgow Central – Manchester Victoria express on 17th July 1965, although by this date Bank Hall depot had closed.

*John Whiteley*

No. 45698 *Mars* is shown again, this time passing the site of Wreay station on 31st July 1965, heading the 2pm Saturdays only Glasgow – Manchester Victoria express.

*R. H. Leslie*

*Right* No. 45578 *United Provinces* working hard between Clifton and Thrimby Grange on an 'up' Saturdays only express on 29th August 1959.

*Gavin Morrison*

*Below* Climbing towards Thrimby Grange near Little Strickland with an 'up' parcels train, is a very dirty No. 45664 *Nelson* on 13th April 1963.

*John Whiteley*

*Left* This picture shows the south end of Penrith station to advantage in 1962, with No. 45703 *Thunderer* heading an 'up' mixed freight on 9th June.

*John Whiteley*

*Above* Drifting down the hill into Penrith with a full head of steam is No. 45702 *Colossus* heading the 8.40am Manchester Victoria – Glasgow Central on 31st July 1958.

*R. H. Leslie*

*Left* No. 45715 *Invincible* makes a spectacular departure from Carlisle with the 'up' 9.50am Edinburgh Waverley to Nottingham train on 29th July 1961.

*R. H. Leslie*

# Freight Workings

*Right* After they were no longer required for main line duties at Holbeck depot, a few of the 'Jubilees', which had been at that depot for many years, were transferred to Low Moor and Wakefield for local freight and parcels duties during the week, with workings to either the east or west coast resorts at weekends. No. 45565 *Victoria* and No. 45694 *Bellerophon* were based at Low Moor, and *Victoria* is seen coming off the Cleckheaton line at Thornhill with a rake of empty wagons from Spen Valley to Healey Mills on 13th October 1962.
*John Whiteley*

*Below* Climbing up the 1 in 50 from Shipley on the line via Idle to Quarry Gap at Laisterdyke, is No. 45694 *Bellerophon* as it passes Shipley Junction signal box, and a Great Northern somersault signal, on 7th July 1964. The two locomotives based at Low Moor at this period were always well groomed,
*Gavin Morrison*

*Left* Sometime in 1964 No. 45604 *Ceylon* is seen passing Kilburn High Road with a fast fitted freight from Camden to Carlisle.

M. Welch

*Right* Drifting down the hill from Hellifield to Skipton just north of Bell Busk is No. 45585 *Hyderabad* with a long freight on 14th October 1961.

Gavin Morrison

*Below* Many 'Jubilees' finished their working days based at Burton-on-Trent on freight duties along the Midland main lines. No. 45618 *New Hebrides* was one of these locomotives, and it is seen heading south past Burton-on-Trent on 4th June 1963.

Hugh Ballantyne

*Right* The 13.30 Hunslet, Leeds to Carlisle had No. 45562 *Alberta* in charge on 30th September 1967. This was by special arrangement, as a party of enthusiasts from the West Riding Branch of the Railway Correspondence and Travel Society were travelling in the leading brake-van. The train is passing through Skipton station on its way north. This was the same day that No. 7029 *Clun Castle* travelled north over the Settle – Carlisle line on a special.

*Gavin Morrison*

*Below* On weekdays the Hunslet – Carlisle freight departed at 12.55. No. 45697 *Achilles* was in charge on 15th March 1967, and is just setting off from the 'down' goods line at Skipton South. At this time the locomotive was running with a lined black tender from one of the withdrawn Holbeck Class 5s.

*Gavin Morrison*

*Above* No. 45732 *Sanspareil* heads an 'up' freight at Plumpton on 3rd March 1952. After withdrawal in February 1964, this locomotive was cut up in the sidings at Otley station in Yorkshire.

*R. H. Leslie*

*Below* No. 45675 *Hardy* travels under the wires of the then electrified line from Morecambe to Lancaster. The train is approaching Scale Halt, and is the 14.53 Heysham to Stourton, Leeds on Saturday, 9th October 1965.

*Gavin Morrison*

*Right* In June 1966, Holbeck 'Jubilee' No. 45675 *Hardy* leaves Bradford Forster Square for Heysham on the 15.17 parcels.

*John Whiteley*

*Below* Just ex-Crewe Works, No. 45668 *Madden* of Patricroft depot, Manchester leaves Rugby with an 'up' van train in June 1962.

*J. B. C. McCann*

*Above Right* The 16.20 Stourton – Carnforth freight passes Wortley Junction, Leeds, headed by No. 45697 *Achilles* on 25th August 1967.

*Gavin Morrison*

*Right* At Mile Post 25 on the West Coast Main Line north of Hemel Hempstead, No. 45740 *Munster* raises the echoes with a 'down' fast fitted freight, as a 'Duchess' Pacific rapidly catches up with an express in 1959. Note the neatness of the ballast and cess which had been specially prepared for publicity purposes.

*M. Welch*

# On the Settle – Carlisle Line

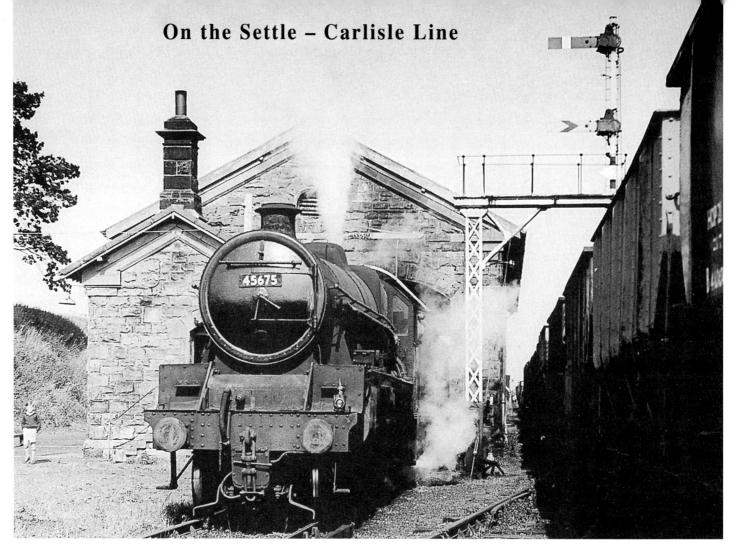

*Above* Not the normal motive power for the Appleby pick up freight, but in May 1967 No. 45675 *Hardy* was photographed in the goods shed at Appleby West.

P. Walton

*Below* The Saturday afternoon van train from Bradford Forster Square to Heysham is passed by an 'up' freight between Long Preston and Settle Junction as it heads north with No. 45647 *Sturdee* in charge on 18th March 1967. This locomotive was withdrawn the following month.

*Gavin Morrison*

*Right* Early on a May morning in 1967 No. 45675 *Hardy* makes an all out effort to get an 'up' freight on the move from Appleby West.

P. Walton

*Below* On 24th May 1960, the 3.40pm stopping train from Bradford Forster Square to Carlisle had Kingmoor allocated No. 45730 *Ocean* in charge. Nearing the end of its journey it is leaving Armathwaite. During the last few years of steam operation at Kingmoor, this train became well known to enthusiasts, as it was often hauled by the last 'Royal Scots' and 'Britannias'.

R. H. Leslie

*Above* The summer Saturdays only from Heads of Ayr to Leeds is approaching Ais Gill Summit on a hot 1st September 1962, headed by the last 'Jubilee' built, No. 45742 *Connaught*, at the time allocated to Kingmoor.

*Gavin Morrison*

*Above right* The relief to the 'up' "Thames – Clyde Express" is seen passing Ais Gill Summit on 16th July 1960 with No. 45697 *Achilles* in charge, in terrible external condition, and still attached to the 3,500 gallon Fowler tender.

*Gavin Morrison*

*Above* Wild Boar Fell dominates the background to this picture of No. 45562 *Alberta* approaching the summit at Ais Gill, hauling the 'up' "Waverley" express on 13th May 1961. Note the 12-wheeled dining car, which is the fourth coach.

*Gavin Morrison*

*Left* Another view of the same train on the same day as the picture above was taken only 200 yards down the track. Neither photographer was aware of the other's presence as it was more usual to have the summit to one's self on a summer Saturday afternoon in 1961!

*R. H. Leslie*

*Right* This picture captures the atmosphere on a dull wet day at Appleby West in the winter months of 1966, as No. 45647 *Sturdee*, showing a Farnley Junction shed plate, pauses on the 'down' 13.32 local to Carlisle.

*P. Walton*

*Left* No. 45660 *Rooke* takes water at Appleby West in 1966 as it prepares to head south with a freight for Stourton. In October 1937 this locomotive was chosen for dynamometer-car trials over the Settle – Carlisle line to test the capability of the 24-element superheater, vertical throatplate boiler. The performance was impressive on the southbound test, as the 48.4 miles from Carlisle to Ais Gill Summit were covered at an average speed of 60 mph with a load of 302 tons.

*P. Walton*

*Right* No. 45562 *Alberta* climbs steadily up the 1 in 100 just north of Horton in Ribblesdale on 30th September 1967 on the 13.30 Stourton – Carlisle freight.

*John Whiteley*

# Around Chester, Shrewsbury and North Wales

*Left* Edge Hill, Liverpool based, No. 45671 *Prince Rupert* is seen dead on Llandudno Junction shed on Sunday 31st March 1963.

*Gavin Morrison*

*Right* The turntable at Llandudno was a busy place on summer Saturdays, and No. 45558 *Manitoba* is just about to be turned before backing on to its stock for the return excursion working to Manchester Exchange on 22nd June 1963.

*Gavin Morrison*

*Below* The track layout at the east end of Llandudno Junction has not altered a lot in 26 years, other than the diamond crossover, signals and signal box which have gone. On 22nd June 1963 No. 45592 *Indore*, a Carnforth based locomotive, leaves with an 'up' express.

*Gavin Morrison*

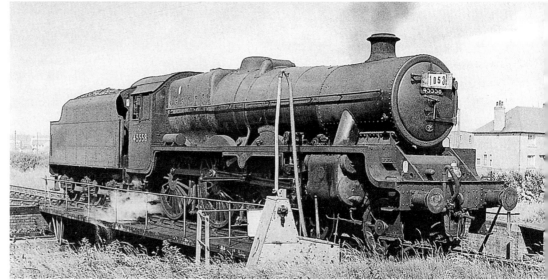

*Right* No. 45699 *Galatea* leaves Chester General, under one of the famous LNWR signal gantries, with an 'up' express from Birkenhead to Paddington on 30th May 1964.

*John Whiteley*

*Left* No. 45699 *Galatea* emerges from under the bridges of Chester Northgate station with a 'down' express on 30th May 1964. The locomotive is now stored at Tyseley Locomotive Works.

*John Whiteley*

*Below* A 'down' fitted freight heads west out of Chester General for North Wales on 30th May 1964 headed by No. 45606 *Falkland Islands*.

*John Whiteley*

*Left* No. 45577 *Bengal* blows off under the overall roof at Shrewsbury as it prepares to leave with the 4.30pm Birkenhead – Paddington on 23rd June 1962.

*John Whiteley*

*Right* A sharp contrast to the west end of Shrewsbury today, this picture shows the old station roof and water tower, as No. 45577 *Bengal* leaves with the 4.30pm Birkenhead - Paddington train.

*John Whiteley*

*Below* The skyline is dominated by the castle. as No. 45554 *Ontario* in ex-works condition from a visit to Crewe, passes under the well-known and much photographed gantry at the east end of Shrewsbury station on 23rd June 1962. The train is the 8.40 am Cardiff - Manchester.

*John Whiteley*

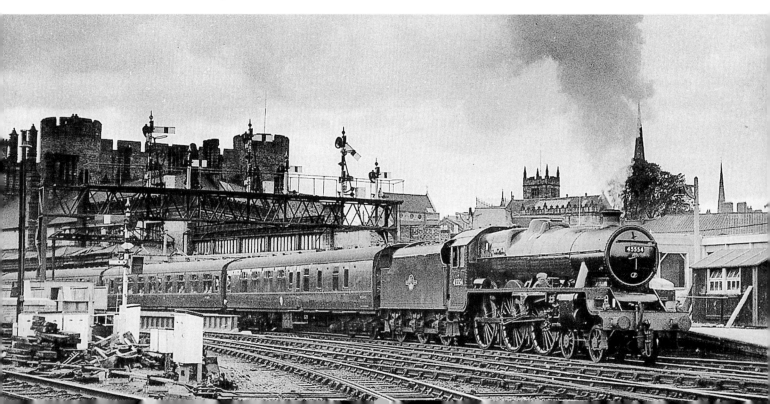

*Right* A semi-fast train from Shrewsbury to Stafford is leaving Wellington on 30th August 1952 headed by No. 45740 *Munster*.

*Brian Morrison*

*Below* A fine study at the best-known photographic location at Shrewsbury station shows No. 45595 *Southern Rhodesia* restarting a Paignton – Liverpool express on 21st July 1954. Note the large crest above the nameplate. One of these nameplates changed hands in the late 1980s for over £16,000!

*Brian Morrison*

# Trans Pennine Services

*Opposite top* Holbeck's No. 45593 *Kolhapur* is approaching Longwood as it makes a spirited climb from Huddersfield to Standedge with a Saturdays only Newcastle to Llandudno train on 8th July 1967.

*Gavin Morrison*

*Above* Farnley Junction based No. 45581 *Bihar and Orissa* gets away from Liverpool at Edge Hill with a Newcastle express on 22nd August 1955.

*Brian Morrison*

*Below* After leaving Manchester Exchange No. 45695 *Minotaur* accelerates through Manchester Victoria before tackling Miles Platting Bank in 1957, with an express for Newcastle or Hull. The train was being assisted at the rear by 2P class 4-4-0 No. 40635 of Patricroft shed, which performed this duty for many years. Ivatt 2-6-0 No. 46437 is behind the 'Jubilee'.

*M. Welch*

*Opposite below* Bank Hall's No. 45698 *Mars* is in charge of a football special taking Everton fans for a game at Elland Road, Leeds on 25th January 1964, and is seen approaching the end of the long climb from Manchester at Diggle. The two far tracks are for the Micklehurst loop line from Stalybridge which closed in 1966.

*Gavin Morrison*

*Left* No. 45558 *Manitoba* of Patricroft depot Manchester, emerges from Huddersfield Tunnel and passes Springwood Junction before entering Gledholt Tunnel with a Leeds – Manchester local train on 24th May 1959.

*Gavin Morrison*

*Below* The 4pm Hull – Liverpool Lime Street express is seen storming past Bradley Junction, east of Huddersfield on 26th June 1960 with No. 45708 *Resolution*, a Farnley Junction locomotive for many post war years. There was once a station at this site which closed in 1950. The cross overs just to the left of the signal box were for the curve onto the Calder Valley line.

*Gavin Morrison*

*Above* No. 45593 *Kolhapur* at Mirfield station on 19th September 1966 when the station still had a roof, on the afternoon Leeds – Wavertree parcels train.

*Below* No. 45593 *Kolhapur* climbs the steep curve out of Leeds on the summer Saturdays only Newcastle – Llandudno train on 8th July 1967.

*Both Gavin Morrison*

*Left* Carrying out one of its regular duties in the later 1950s and early 1960s, No. 45698 *Mars* of Bank Hall depot, Liverpool passes Hebden Bridge with the 10.30am Liverpool Exchange to Newcastle train on 27th February 1960.

*Gavin Morrison*

*Below* A Sunday special from Leeds to Blackpool hurries through the very deep cutting before Luddendenfoot on 19th June 1966, behind Low Moor allocated No. 45565 *Victoria*.

*Gavin Morrison*

*Above* A summer Saturday extra from Bradford Exchange to Blackpool passes Luddendenfoot headed by No. 45565 *Victoria* on 18th June 1966. The station closed on 8th September 1962.

*Gavin Morrison*

*Below* The famous Heaton to Red Bank Manchester empty van train, which was hauled by a wide variety of locomotives in the 1950s and '60s passes Sowerby Bridge on 29th June 1964, when Newton Heath 'Jubilee' No. 45710 *Irresistible* was piloting Class 5 No. 45294 from the same depot. On the far right is the track which used to form the branch to Rishworth but this had closed to all traffic in 1953.

*Gavin Morrison*

*Left* No. 45565 *Victoria* returning home to Bradford with the out and back summer Saturday working to Blackpool on 9th July 1966. The picture was taken near Copley, between Milner Royd Junction and Dryclough Junction on the Halifax line.

*Gavin Morrison*

*Below* An interesting view of Halifax Town station on 20th August 1966 with Fowler 2-6-4T No. 42410 having just arrived with the Leeds portion of an excursion for Bridlington, while Low Moor's No. 45565 *Victoria* has come from Bradford Exchange. After No. 42410 has uncoupled, *Victoria* will combine the two portions of the train.

*P. Walton*

*Right* The crew of No. 45565 *Victoria* put up a good exhaust for the benefit of the photographer as they leave Leeds Central and approach Holbeck High Level with a summer Saturdays only train to Blackpool on 20th August 1966.
*Gavin Morrison*

*Below* One of Bank Hall's trio of 'Jubilees' at the time, No. 45717 *Dauntless* arrives at Brighouse station on the 10.30am Liverpool Exchange to Newcastle express on 12th July 1960. The station closed on 3rd January 1970, although it has subsequently been re-opened.
*Gavin Morrison*

# North of Carlisle

No. 45624 *St. Helena* and No. 45712 *Victory* at the head of a Glasgow – Manchester Victoria express have just arrived at Carlisle. The locomotives are standing a few yards to the rear of the preceding train, already in the station. Platform space at Carlisle was at a premium on summer Saturdays in the early 1950s, and although only the two leading coaches are at the platform, passengers are already alighting. This picture was taken in August 1952.

*R. H. Leslie*

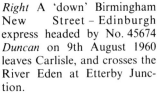

*Right* A 'down' Birmingham New Street – Edinburgh express headed by No. 45674 *Duncan* on 9th August 1960 leaves Carlisle, and crosses the River Eden at Etterby Junction.

*Gavin Morrison*

*Left* A northbound freight with No. 45732 *Sanspareil* of Kingmoor shed in charge, passes Dumfries on 29th June 1957.

*Brian Morrison*

*Above* Stanier 2-6-4T No. 42594 provides assistance for Newton Heath's No. 45635 *Tobago* for the climb to Shap with the 10.50am Glasgow to Manchester and Liverpool on 27th February 1960, as they leave Carlisle.

*R. H. Leslie*

*Below* Perth based member of the class, No. 45727 *Inflexible* prepares to depart from Edinburgh Waverley with the 10.12am departure for Inverness on 1st July 1957, which it would work as far as Perth.

*J. P. Wilson*

*Left* Storming up the bank as it approaches Dunblane No. 45691 *Orion* of Kingmoor, heads north with a mixed van train for Perth and beyond on 13th June 1959.

*Gavin Morrison*

*Right* No. 45673 *Keppel* of Perth shed arrives at Aberdeen with the 'down' West Coast postal working on 19th April 1954. The coaches on this train had to be turned every day on the Ferryhill depot turntable, although occasionally they were taken to Kittybrewster.

*J. B. C. McCann*

*Left* An 'up' express for Manchester leaves Perth in fine style, past the shed coaler on 24th June 1957, headed by Kingmoor based No. 45715 *Invincible*.

*Brian Morrison*

# Double-Heading

*Above* A pre-war picture of No. 5601 *British Guiana*, rather unusually acting as pilot to an unidentified Midland 2P class 4-4-0 near Headstone Lane with an 'up' Northampton – Euston local train in 1938.

*C. R. L. Coles*

*Below* The amount of railway interest in this picture is remarkable. On 4th June 1938, LMS 2P class 4-4-0 No. 450 is piloting 'Jubilee' No. 5621 *Northern Rhodesia* near Long Eaton, with a St Pancras – Leeds and Bradford Forster Square express.

*J. P. Wilson*

*Above* Super power for the "Mid-day Scot" on 28th April 1956. No. 45613 *Kenya*, running with one of the Fowler high, straight-sided tenders, pilots 'Princess Royal' class 4-6-2 No. 46206 *Princess Marie Louise* just south of Eden Valley Junction at the start of the final southbound climb to Shap Summit.

*R. H. Leslie*

*Below* Power to spare for the 10am Newcastle – Liverpool Lime Street to tackle the climb over the Pennines. Rebuilt 'Jubilee' No. 45736 *Phoenix* pilots rebuilt 'Royal Scot' No. 46124 *London Scottish* out of Leeds past Farnley Junction shed, which can be seen on the extreme left hand side of the picture, taken on 27th February 1960.

*Gavin Morrison*

*Right* Wintry conditions in 1958 surround No. 45671 *Prince Rupert* and an unidentified rebuilt 'Royal Scot' as they pass through Macclesfield Central with the 'up' 2.05pm Manchester London Road to Euston. Note the dmu in the old British Railways green livery on the left.
*M. Welch*

*Left* The Heaton – Red Bank vans was always double-headed and produced a wide variety of motive power over the postwar years. On 9th September 1963 a fairly regular combination of 'Jubilee' and Class 5 produced No. 45581 *Bihar and Orissa* and No. 45428. The Class 5 is now preserved on the North Yorkshire Moors Railway. The location is Farnley Junction, Leeds; the shed coaler is visible above the bridge in the background.
*Gavin Morrison*

*Right* Another view of the Heaton – Red Bank vans on 30th April 1966 at Farnley Junction, Leeds, when the last active 'Jubilee' on the London Midland Region, No. 45627 *Sierra Leone* was piloting Class 5 No. 45336. The 'Jubilee' was withdrawn in September 1966.
*Gavin Morrison*

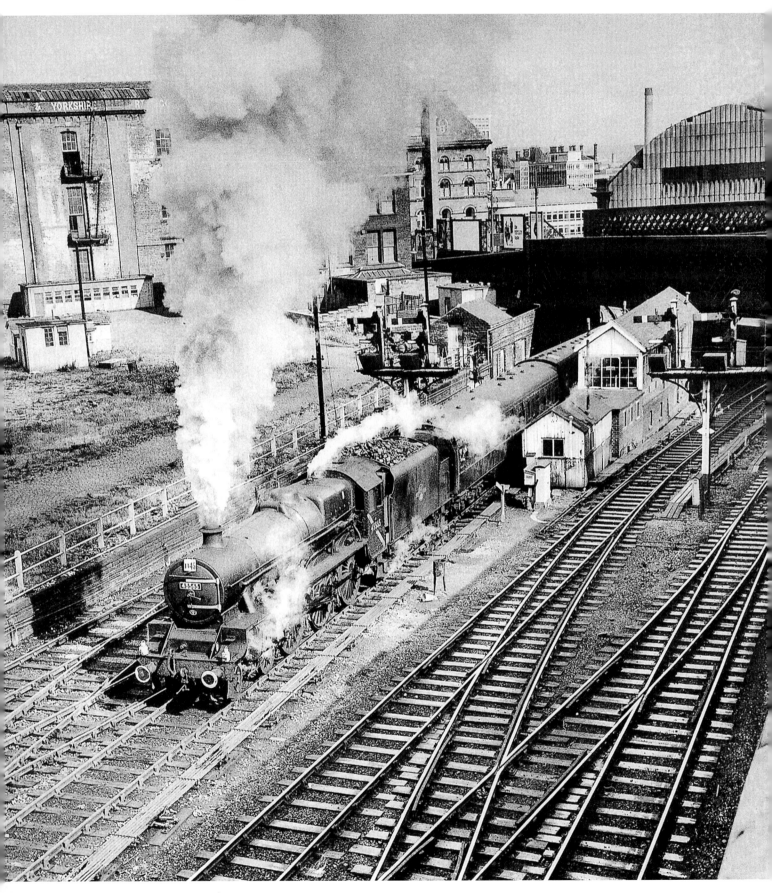

Passing the site where the present platforms of Bradford Interchange station end, is No. 45565 *Victoria* making a vigorous departure up the 1 in 50 gradient to Bowling Junction on 21st August 1966 with a special to Blackpool.

*Gavin Morrison*

*Right* The section of the line from Laisterdyke to Bowling Junction on the outskirts of Bradford closed completely in 1985, although regular stopping trains had ceased on 31st December 1961. On 9th July 1966, when it was still a through route, a Leeds Central – Blackpool special headed by No. 45565 *Victoria* is seen on this section.

*Gavin Morrison*

*Left* No. 45697 *Achilles*, running attached to a lined black tender from a Class 5, struggles over the summit of the 1 in 50 climb out of Bradford with a Bradford Exchange to Blackpool express on 10th June 1967. The location is Bowling Junction, the 2-6-4T banking the train is out of sight, and the line to the right is to Laisterdyke as mentioned in the caption above.

*Gavin Morrison*

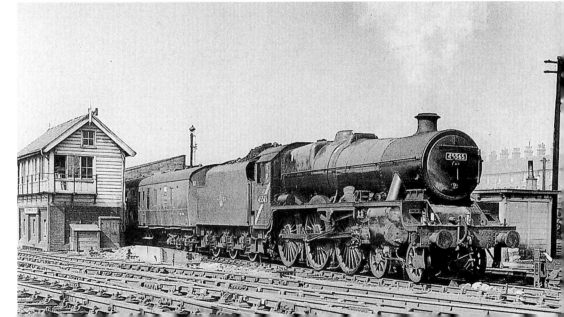

*Right* No. 45565 *Victoria* pulls empty carriage stock past Low Moor shed, en route to Bradford Exchange, prior to it being worked to Blackpool on 31st May 1966.

*Gavin Morrison*

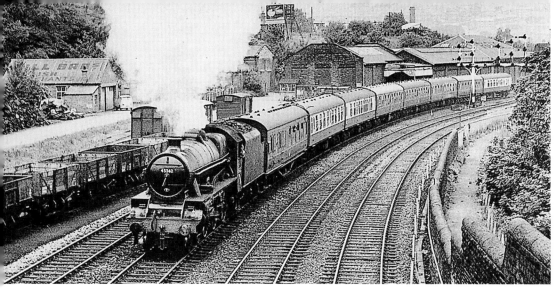

*Left* A special from Morecambe to Bradford Forster Square worked by No. 45562 *Alberta*, pulls away from a stop at Shipley on the last stage of its journey on 1st July 1967.

*John Whiteley*

*Below* On a wintry 1st February 1963 the 'up' "Devonian" leaves Bradford Forster Square powered by Holbeck based No. 45608 *Gibraltar*.

*John Whiteley*

*Below left* The afternoon train for Heysham is ready to leave Bradford Forster Square on 29th April 1967 with No. 45697 *Achilles* in charge. The locomotive is in unlined green livery with diagonal yellow stripe on the cabside, together with a lined black tender from a withdrawn Class 5.

*Gavin Morrison*

*Below right* No. 45697 *Achilles* on the Heysham van train on the same day as the previous picture makes a spirited departure from Bradford Forster Square.

*F. J. Bullock*

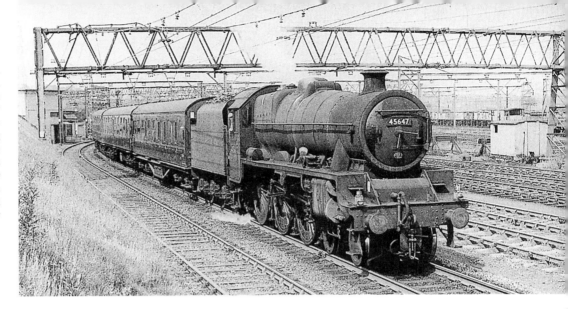

*Right* The Penistone line from Huddersfield to Barnsley had a regular visit in the mid-1960s from a 'Jubilee' on summer Saturdays, the Leeds and Bradford to Poole being diagrammed regularly for the class. The three pictures on this page show No. 45647 *Sturdee* on the outward and return workings. This picture shows it leaving Penistone for Barnsley under the wires.

*Right* No. 45647 *Sturdee* leaves Penistone across the magnificent viaduct towards Huddersfield on the return Poole – Bradford working.

*Right* No. 45647 *Sturdee* had negotiated successfully the steep 1 in 50 climb out of Barnsley to Summer Lane and is seen blasting its way up the 1 in 90 past Dodworth. The rest of the climb at 1 in 100 to Penistone allowed the photographer plenty of time to get to Penistone and take the picture above.

*All Gavin Morrison*

# South of Birmingham

*Left* No. 45590 *Travancore*, showing a 19B shed plate indicating it was allocated to Sheffield Millhouses depot at the time, stands in the centre road at Bristol Temple Meads in July 1953.

*C. R. L. Coles*

*Below* Bristol Barrow Road based No. 45602 *British Honduras* approaches the right-angled crossing at Ashchurch with an express from the Midlands on 9th July 1955. The Midland signal on the left is well featured.

*Hugh Ballantyne*

*Above* A summer Saturday extra from the Midlands arrives at Bath, headed by No. 45647 *Sturdee* when it was still allocated to a Birmingham shed.

*Hugh Ballantyne*

*Below* The 10.05am Bournemouth West to Bradford starts the second stage of its journey north from Bath Green Park, having travelled over the Somerset and Dorset line. No. 45562 *Alberta* is in charge, and being Holbeck based was most likely working through to Leeds City on 4th August 1962.

*Hugh Ballantyne*

# Workings out of Leeds

*Left* No. 45593 *Kolhapur* is ready to leave Leeds City with the afternoon van train for Wavertree, Liverpool. The locomotive is well groomed as Partick Whitehouse, who purchased the locomotive for preservation, was travelling on the footplate. The date was 19th September 1966.

*Gavin Morrison*

*Below* Carnforth depot in the early 1960s did not seem to have any cleaners to look after their batch of 'Jubilees'. No. 45606 *Falkland Islands* leaves Leeds City on the 12th May 1961 with the 1.54pm departure for Carnforth, as a brand new 'Peak' class diesel waits to leave the platform, on the right.

*Gavin Morrison*

*Above* No. 45619 *Nigeria* was the first of the regular Holbeck 'Jubilees' to be withdrawn, in August 1961. Looking rather run down, two months before the end, it is seen leaving Leeds on the 5.20pm to Bristol on 2nd June.

*Gavin Morrison*

*Below* The 16.50 all-stations, Leeds Central to Doncaster, became a regular 'Jubilee' working in 1965. No. 45574 *India* passes the site of Beeston station on 28th June 1965.

*Gavin Morrison*

*Above* A light load for No. 45660 *Rooke*, as it passes White-hall Junction, Leeds and heads for Morecambe on 31st July 1965.

*John Whiteley*

*Above* No. 45593 *Kolhapur* storms up the four-track section to Cross Gates, Leeds on a special on 22nd April 1967. In 1966 and 1967 this locomotive ran with a leaking middle cylinder, and ruined many enthusiasts' photographs, as is seen in this picture.

*Gavin Morrison*

*Below* Empty carriage stock from Neville Hill sidings, Leeds leaves for City station with No. 45562 *Alberta* on 16th September 1966, the stock being required for a special to Blackpool.

*Gavin Morrison*

# Withdrawn and in Store

*Left* Dumped at Newton Heath depot on 23rd March 1963 is No. 45706 *Express* still with nameplate attached, together with No. 45702 *Colossus*, No. 45701 *Conqueror* (all allocated to the depot for many years), plus 2-6-4T No. 42698, rebuilt 'Royal Scot' No. 46133 *The Green Howards*, and 'Jubilee' No. 45679 *Armada*.
*Gavin Morrison*

*Right* Part of the line up shown in the picture above is No. 45701 *Conqueror* at Newton Heath depot on 23rd March 1963.

*Gavin Morrison*

*Left* Not very long out of works after overhaul, No. 45640 *Frobisher* was stored at Carlisle Kingmoor, but was withdrawn in March 1964. The picture was taken in the following month.

*Gavin Morrison*

# Jubilees Before and After Preservation

*Above* No. 45690 *Leander* was a regular visitor to York when it was based at Bristol Barrow Road in the 1950s and early 1960. It is at the south end of the station ready to depart with an 'up' express on 22nd May 1959, with Class A2/3 Pacific No. 60513 *Dante* ready to head south.

*Brian Morrison*

*Below* The motive power surrounding No. 45690 *Leander* on 16th June 1962 does not suggest the picture was taken on the ash pits at York shed, as there is not an Eastern Region locomotive in sight!

*Gavin Morrison*

*Right* No. 5690 *Leander* climbing steadily to Chinley at Buxworth on 24th February 1979 at the head of a special from Guide Bridge to York and then to Carnforth.

*John Whiteley*

*Below* On 21st February 1979 No. 5690 *Leander* worked a special from Dinting to York. The train is seen passing Burton Salmon, when the signals and junction were still intact.

*Gavin Morrison*

*Above* The Saturdays only 10.17 Leeds – Glasgow will always be associated with the last of the 'Jubilees', as it was one of their final regular main line passenger workings. No. 45593 *Kolhapur* storms past Whitehall Junction, Leeds on 5th August 1967.

*John Whiteley*

*Above* No. 5593 *Kolhapur*, heading south over the Settle and Carlisle line near Ormside, with the southbound "Mancunian" special on 18th April 1987. This route was frequently traversed by the locomotive during its last few years of operation, when based at Holbeck, Leeds.

*John Whiteley*

*Below* Another picture of No. 5593 *Kolhapur* getting into its stride with the 'down' "Cumbrian Mountain Express" on the outskirts of Leeds, just before passing under the ring road at Calverley and Rodley on 21st March 1987.

*Gavin Morrison*

*Above* A humble duty for No. 45596 *Bahamas* on 22nd April 1965, as it shunts some wagons in Copley Hill, London & North Western yard at Leeds, prior to setting off for the Manchester area.

*Gavin Morrison*

*Below* Saturday 12th July 1964 saw No. 45596 *Bahamas* dead on Farnley Junction depot, Leeds. The dirty external condition with painted "9B" on the smokebox is in sharp contrast to the pictures on the opposite page.

*Gavin Morrison*

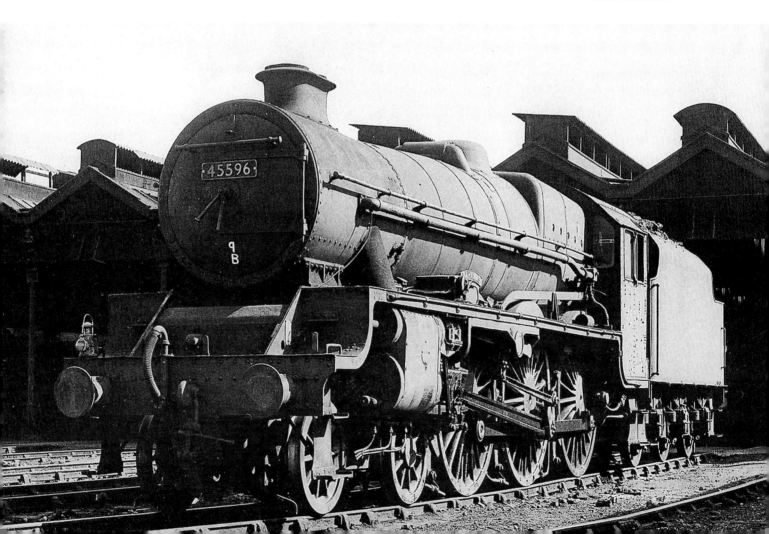

*Above* The locomotive visited Reddish depot Open Day on 9th September 1973, and is just leaving to return to the now closed Dinting Railway Centre with its support coach, 0-6-0ST 'Austerity' *Warrington* and SR 'Schools' class 4-4-0 No. 30925 *Cheltenham*.

*M. Welch*

*Right* During its first short spell of main line running after preservation, No. 5596 *Bahamas* rounds the triangle at Chinley North Junction, with a special to Sheffield on 17th June 1973. The livery was supposed to be the same red as originally applied to the class, but was in fact nearer a "dark pink" colour. Fortunately, in 1989 it appeared on the main line again in authentic BR lined green, the correct livery with its double chimney.

*Gavin Morrison*

*Below* The 'down' "Cumbrian Mountain Express" headed by *Bahamas*, resplendent in its new green livery, is seen near New Biggin on 10th August 1989.

*R. H. Leslie*

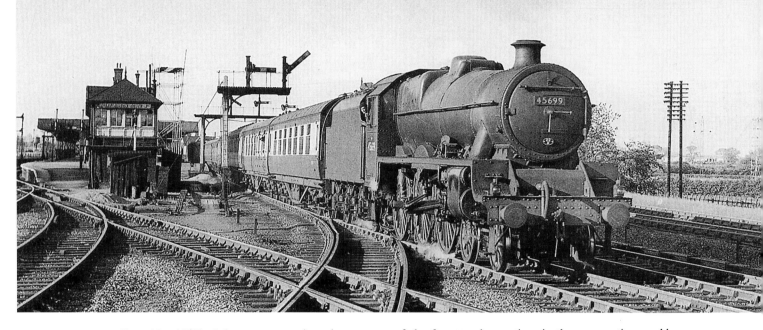

*Above* No. 45699 *Galatea*, seems to have become one of the forgotten locomotives in the preservation world, but in happier times it is seen leaving Trent station with an 'up' Glasgow express on 4th June 1955. The shed plate shows 22A, indicating it was a Bristol locomotive at the time, which probably meant it had been borrowed by Holbeck for the diagram.

*J. P. Wilson*

*Below* A depressing picture of No. 45699 *Galatea* dumped at Steamtown, Carnforth on 5th May 1980. It has since been moved to Tyseley Locomotive Works. Obviously restoration to working order would be a mammoth task (note that centre driving wheel!), but it wouldn't be the first miracle performed by the preservationists. Who knows its future?

*D. Dyson*